Heirloom
MACHINE QUILTING

4TH EDITION

*Comprehensive Guide to Hand-Quilting Effects
Using Your Sewing Machine*

HARRIET HARGRAVE

C&T PUBLISHING

Text © 2004 Harriet Hargrave
Artwork © Harriet Hargrave and C&T Publishing

Publisher: Amy Marson
Editorial Director: Gailen Runge
Editorial team: Gailen Runge, Darra Williamson
Proofreaders: Susan Nelson, Cyndy Lyle Rymer
Cover Designer: Christina D. Jarumay
Design Director/Book Designer: Christina D. Jarumay
Illustrator: Jeff Carrillo
Production Assistant: Kirstie L. McCormick
Photography: Brian Birlauf
Published by C&T Publishing, Inc., P.O. Box 1456, Lafayette, California, 94549

Front cover: *Double Peony*
Back cover: *Friendship Album*

Library of Congress Cataloging-in-Publication Data
Hargrave, Harriet.
 Heirloom machine quilting : comprehensive guide to hand-quilting effects
using your sewing machine / Harriet Hargrave.-- 4th ed.
     p. cm.
 Includes bibliographical references and index.
 ISBN 1-57120-236-6 (hardcover)
 1. Machine quilting. I. Title.

 TT835.H338 2004
 746.46--dc22

                          2004000781

Printed in China
10 9 8 7 6 5 4

Dedication

As always, this book is dedicated to my mother for the love of quilting and sewing that she shared with me throughout my life, and to the many thousands of students who have shared their time with me these past 25 years of teaching. Together we have brought machine quilting to standards of skill that we couldn't have imagined in the beginning.

Acknowledgments

I would like to thank the following people and companies for their contributions to this book:

◙ Charla Gee, for all the long hours spent piecing the blocks for the new quilt tops so I could concentrate on the quilting.

◙ My employees, for running my store without me so I could spend six months writing and quilting.

◙ My students, who continue to excite me in the classroom. When asked if I ever get tired of teaching beginners, I always reply, "NO! How could you get tired of the excitement on their faces when they realize how much fun this is!"

◙ Diane Gaudynski, for inspiring me to push myself to the next level, and for showing the world that the most awesome machine quilting is not coming from huge machines, but is being created by our hands and our best friends—our home-sewing machines.

◙ The quilters who let me photograph their wonderful quilts. I hope their work inspires you to want to pursue this rewarding skill.

◙ Apple Computer Inc., for making the job of writing such a pleasure. I enjoy my new iMac as much as my old faithful Bernina.

◙ Andover Fabrics, for donating fabric for use in the quilts.

◙ Fairfield Processing Corporation, for donating batting to photograph and use.

◙ Hobbs Bonded Fibers, for donating batting to photograph and use.

◙ Mountain Mist/Legett and Platt for donating batting to photograph and use.

◙ P&B Fabrics, for donating fabric for use in the quilts.

◙ Quilters Dream Batting, for donating batting to photograph and use.

◙ Superior Threads, for donating thread to experiment with.

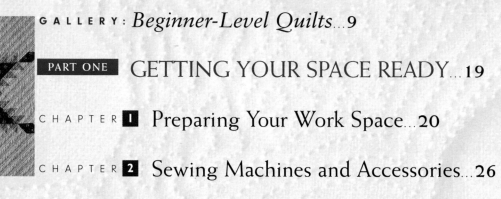

Table of

Contents

Introduction

It's hard to believe that only 22 years ago a major event took place in the quilting world—the revitalization of machine quilting, but in a new form. I am honored and humbled by the part I played in starting such a wonderful activity. My desire for quilts that looked hand-quilted but were done on the sewing machine led me into a world that I couldn't have imagined. Upon mastering free-motion machine embroidery, machine quilting was the next step. With the guidance of my mother, I began exploring the possibilities of adapting machine-embroidery free-motion techniques to the quilting patterns that Mom hand quilted. Introducing invisible nylon thread to this equation gave me the results I was looking for…and the quilts were stunning!

Star Chain, 68" x 68", machine pieced and quilted by Harriet Hargrave. This is the quilt that inspired Marti Michelle to ask Harriet to write the first edition of Heirloom Machine Quilting in 1982. Nylon thread, Mountain Mist 100% Cotton Natural batting.

In 1980, however, machine quilting was a dirty word, and I have to admit that I apologized for it more times than I like to remember. (My local quilt guild did not even allow you to participate in show-and-tell if your project was machine-pieced or quilted.) I find that new quilters generally are not familiar with the history of the revival of machine quilting. We all just take it for granted now. But in the early 1980s, when Marti Michell saw my reproduction quilts and asked me to write a book on my techniques and methods, I felt I was walking into a lion's den. You know the attitude: a quilt is not a real quilt unless it is hand-quilted!

When I started to think about writing a fourth edition of *Heirloom Machine Quilting*, I couldn't wait to add all the information and tips that I have either developed or learned with the help of thousands of students since the release of the third edition in 1995. Often I was asked what I could possibly add. Trust me: I didn't have any problems with subject matter or new information.

This is not a "quick and dirty" quilting book, full of flashy tip boxes but little meat. This is a book that delves into the guts of the topic of machine-quilting technique. It is not a book that can be digested by looking at the pictures. It is a workbook that needs to be read from cover to cover—possibly more than once. It should be at your side during your practice sessions, and used as a constant reference in the future. There is a reason that *Heirloom Machine Quilting* is considered the bible for teaching and learning machine quilting. In your hands you hold 25 years of extensive teaching and quilting experience. Almost every successful machine quilter has been influenced by the previous editions of this book in one way or another.

If you own previous editions of *Heirloom Machine Quilting*, you will notice a lot more step-by-step technique and less behind-the-scenes information in this edition. With all the new information, there just wasn't enough room to do justice to the topics of fabric care, batting, thread science, quilt care, quilt-as-you-go, and so on. Therefore, you will see that information updated and expanded in my next two companion books. In addition, these books will approach the problems of developing quilting ideas for your stored quilt tops, as well as how to think through the sequence of the actual quilting.

I can't help but add a word about longarm machines and the systems that attempt to turn a home machine into a longarm set-up. I am offended that these companies believe they invented machine quilting. I am concerned that beginning machine quilters are being given the impression that they can't quilt a large quilt without a longarm machine, or without investing heavily in the various gimmicks coming on the market. Consumers are being told that machine quilting will wear out their home-sewing machine. I'm here to refute all that nonsense! All the quilts in this book were achieved on small, short-arm home-sewing machines.

More than anything, machine quilting is an attitude and a passion. If you approach the technique with the attitude that it is hard, and you just can't handle the large quilts, you probably can't. You can only do what you tell yourself you can do. If you take the time to adapt your work space to accommodate machine quilting, and sit down behind your machine anticipating the excitement of seeing the finished product in a matter of hours, you will get past the trepidation. It is much like childbirth—the labor is grueling, but the reward at the end wipes all discomfort away in the joy you derive from the final product…and it is all yours! More and more quilters are realizing that when they send a quilt top out to be quilted by someone else, the quilt they get back doesn't feel like it is really "theirs." They may even feel rather detached from it. Unfortunately, we live in a society that expects instant gratification, and we want to try something once and be perfect at it.

Machine quilting does not work that way. It is a learned skill, much like riding a bike or playing the piano. You build one skill on another, and time and practice allow your brain to process the new skill. I find that if you put ten minutes a day into focused practicing for six months, you will become a good quilter in that period of time. If you only give it ten minutes every six months, it's not going to happen. My motto is "buck up" and you can do it. Yes, it can seem difficult, maybe even daunting, but with time and practice, you can create what you see in these photographs, and love doing it on your own machine! Hang in there. The rewards are awesome!

Blue Medallion, 68" x 84", pieced and quilted by Harriet Hargrave. The feathers and elegance of this quilt turned numerous quilters around to thinking that machine quilting could be acceptable—especially Diane Gaudynski. Nylon thread, Mountain Mist 100% polyester batting.

Gallery:
BEGINNER-LEVEL QUILTS

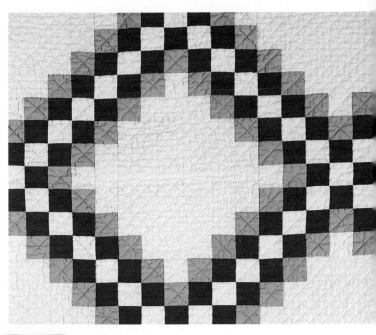

Triple Irish Chain
68" x 90", pieced and quilted by Harriet Hargrave.
This classic traditional quilt is entirely straight-line grid quilted using a walking foot. Hobbs Heirloom Premium cotton-blend batting; Sew-Art International Invisible Nylon clear thread on top; 50/3 Mettler "Silk Finish" (cotton) thread in the bobbin.

Confetti Baskets

59" x 59", pieced and quilted
by Harriet Hargrave.

Straight-line, grid, and simple free-motions techniques.
Adapted from a 1915 quilt made by Susan Anne Basbore
Stouffer. Mountain Mist 100% Cotton Natural batting;
Sew-Art International Invisible Nylon clear thread on top;
50/3 Mettler "Silk Finish" (cotton) thread in the bobbin.

Pilgrim's Progress
69" x 69", pieced and quilted
by Harriet Hargrave.

Ditch, channel, and continuous-curve techniques used.
Hobbs Heirloom Washable Wool batting; combination of
Sew-Art International Invisible nylon smoke-colored thread
and 50/3 Mettler "Silk Finish" cotton thread on top; 50/3
Mettler "Silk Finish" cotton thread in the bobbin.

Sadie's Choice
*50" x 50", machine appliquéd
and quilted by Harriet Hargrave.*

This quilt is ditch quilted around appliqué pieces then echo
quilted using a darning foot. A walking foot was used for
straight seams. Border quilted free-motion. Based on a late
nineteenth-century block pattern. Hobbs Heirloom Premium
cotton-blend batting; combination of Sew-Art International
Invisible nylon clear and 50/3 Mettler "Silk Finish" (cotton)
thread on top; 50/3 Mettler "Silk Finish" (cotton) thread in the
bobbin.

Fleur de Nine
*85" x 95", machine pieced,
hand appliquéd, and machine
quilted by Julie Yaeger Lambert,
Erlanger, KY.*
Ditch, channel, grid and free-motion techniques
used. Border inspired by Kathy Munkelwitz.
Hobbs Heirloom Organic with Scrim cotton
batting; YLI Wonder Invisible Thread on top;
60/2 Mettler cotton embroidery thread in the bobbin.

ADVANCED-BEGINNER
Gallery

Young Man's Fancy
63" x 63", Pieced by Charla Gee, Littleton, CO. and quilted by Harriet Hargrave.

Harriet used a walking foot for ditch and straight-line quilting and free-motion techniques for the patterns. Reproduced from an 1830 indigo-and-white quilt by Content Newton. Hobbs Heirloom Premium cotton-blend batting; Sew-Art International Invisible nylon smoke-colored thread in indigo areas; 50/2 DMC cotton embroidery thread in cream areas and in the bobbin.

Tobacco Worm
53" x 53", pieced and quilted by
Harriet Hargrave.

Based on a pattern from Civil War Women by Barbara
Brackman (C&T Publishing, 2000). The triple-line channels, ditch, and grid quilting were done with a walking
foot; the feathers used free-motion techniques. Harriet
made this quilt to duplicate the original, rather than
with the all-over meandering of the pictured version.
Hobbs Washable Wool batting; Sew-Art International
Invisible Nylon clear thread on top; 50/2 DMC cotton
embroidery thread in the bobbin.

First Feather

29" x 29", pieced and quilted by
Cynthia Schmitz, Arlington Heights, IL.
Fairfield Cotton Classic batting; Quilters Dream
Poly batting for the trapunto; invisible nylon thread
on top; Madeira Tanne 50/2 cotton embroidery
thread in the bobbin.

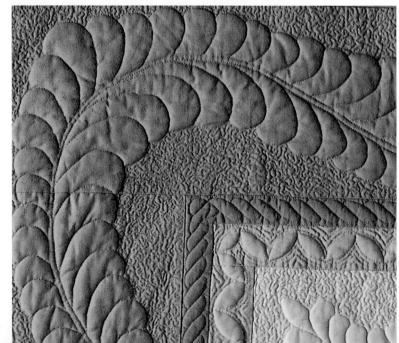

Table Runner

16" x 48", pieced and quilted by Cynthia Schmitz of Arlington Heights, IL.

Fairfield Cotton Classic batting; Quilters Dream Poly batting for trapunto; invisible nylon thread on top; Madeira Tanne 50/2 cotton embroidery thread in the bobbin.

Feathered Variable Star

64" x 64", Pieced by Nancy Barrett, Edmond, OK and quilted by Harriet Hargrave.

This quilt uses limited ditch quilting, free-motion, stippling, and continuous-curve techniques. Hobbs Heirloom Premium cotton-blend batting; 50/2 DMC and 30/2 Mettler cotton embroidery threads on top; 50/2 DMC cotton embroidery thread in the bobbin.

PART ONE

GETTING YOUR SPACE READY

Preparing Your Work Space

I know that for a new quilter, reading all these words can be daunting. The natural reaction is to skip over the first few chapters and get right to the "meat" of the subject—how to do the actual quilting. You may even want to skip the text entirely and just "read" the pictures. As tempting as that is, I hope you'll take the time to go through this information and make the needed adaptations to your work space so your beginning machine quilting experiences are positive ones. I remember the adverse conditions I worked in years ago, when I was first developing these techniques, and the aches and pains that followed. It took years to learn that my enjoyment of quilting large quilts was directly related to how I set up my work space. Be patient: everything you do in the beginning will pay tremendous dividends in the near future. The time you spend practicing will be more efficient, and your level of success greater, if your work space is adapted to machine quilting.

Whenever anyone tells me they find machine quilting difficult, the first thing I ask is how they've set up their sewing machine and work space. I find this is *the* most overlooked aspect of machine quilting and can cause the most frustration in handling any quilt, large or small.

Since the early 1980s, my motto has been: *I do not machine quilt, I hand quilt with an electric needle.* When you think about machine quilting in this way, you will understand why your work space is so important.

Your Sewing Surface

One of the most important considerations for your workroom is providing a cabinet or large extension table for your machine. If you simply set your machine on a table top, you do not have enough support for the bulk of the quilt. The quilt tends to fall off the left side and back of the machine, or get caught at the front edge. As a result, you must use your hands to support the bulk to avoid stress on the needle as you quilt. If your hands are occupied with supporting the quilt, they cannot be at the needle creating the quilting stitches. You must support that bulk with an even, flat surface in order for your hands to be free.

Another problem with a table-top arrangement is the lack of space for your hands to guide the fabric where it must be for quilting. Your fingers may fall off the edges of the machine, hindering your ability to make even, consistent stitches. As a result, you'll begin to tighten up in anticipation of falling off the edge and losing control as you stitch. When you lower the machine into a cabinet, the table surface is level with the throat plate of the machine. The table supports the quilt, leaving your hands free to manipulate the quilt under the needle.

Practice quilting in your current arrangement, and you'll begin to identify any problems with your setup.

SEWING CABINETS

Before you rush out and buy, take some time and do your homework. Go shopping and look at machine cabinets objectively. Often products labeled for "quilting" are really not what you need. Leave your checkbook and credit cards at home, but do take a notebook and tape measure with you. Visit every sewing machine dealer you can and examine and sit at every cabinet they offer. Here is my checklist of things to consider:

◼ Sit in a good chair and move up to the machine. Consider the space provided for you to position yourself in front of the machine. Often this area is too small or positioned incorrectly for you to have good vision while quilting. Can you sit in an ergonomically correct posture and still reach the machine? Can you comfortably reach the foot control?

◼ Sit at different cabinets to find the height most comfortable for you. Are your feet comfortably flat on the floor? Are your arms at your sides, elbows at a 90° angle, and wrists resting on the cabinet top? Are your shoulders relaxed? Are you sitting high enough to see down the front of the machine and into the hole in the throat plate where the needle enters? I personally like my hands to be a bit lower than my elbows, at about a 100° to 110° angle. Machine cabinets generally run 28" to 30" in height (from the bed of the machine to the floor). If the cabinet is too high, you'll need to reach up or lift up your chair. If the cabinet is too low, you won't be able to sit close enough to the machine. To compensate, you'll probably move the chair back and sit on the edge—a position that quickly causes fatigue.

◼ Can you sit directly in front of the needle? Many cabinets center you with the machine, requiring you to twist slightly to the left to control the fabric going through the machine. You'll definitely want to avoid this arrangement. It places undue stress on your back and shoulders, distorts your vision, and generally makes the quilting process more difficult. Remember that quilting is mainly eye/hand coordination, and if you aren't centered with the needle, it is harder to coordinate your eyes with your hands.

◼ How much workspace do you have on the cabinet top? I like to have three to four feet to my left, and four to five feet behind the machine. If you need to, you can extend the working surface by placing additional tables around the cabinet. Place one behind the machine and one to the left of the cabinet so the quilt is supported and cannot fall onto the floor and drag against the needle as you quilt.

◼ Study the transitions between the machine arm, the insert, and the cabinet top. There should be a perfectly smooth transition from one to the other. If there is any offset edge, your fingers will run into it and cause a stutter in your stitching—the last thing you want when you are quilting that marvelous double-stitched feather! Also check the insert material. I like an insert made from the same material as the cabinet top—generally a laminate such as Formica. Many inserts are now made of acrylic, which can cause the fabric to drag while you are quilting. You may want to have a custom insert made once you choose your cabinet.

◼ Is the needle more that six inches away from the edge of the work surface so you can stitch with control and comfort? Can you lean forward, rest your forearms on the edge of the cabinet, relax your hands over the fabric, and still see the needle entering the machine clearly? To avoid carpel tunnel syndrome, your wrists and fingertips should be slightly lower than your elbows.

> *Tip*
>
> Once you've determined a comfortable setup, have an insert custom cut to accommodate the new machine position if necessary.

This is a good time to consider the needle-bar placement on your machine. Many newer embroidery machines have a redesigned needle-bar position, pushing it to the back of the machine, instead of forward or centered in the head. This can cause vision problems without you even realizing it. If you are sitting comfortably in front of the machine, but can't see the needle, you may have a problem with stitch control and accuracy in your quilting.

Large work surface suitable for machine quilting

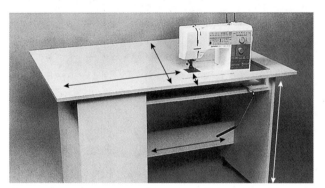

Important measurements for personalizing a machine cabinet

EXTENSION TABLES FOR SEWING

If owning a cabinet is not feasible for you, you have an inexpensive, portable alternative. Consider having an extension table custom made from $3/4$" particle-board, laminate-covered countertop material. If need be, the extension can be as large as your table surface. Look for a product with a smooth surface (for example, laminate) that allows the fabric to glide easily. Avoid wood, as fabric tends to drag and wood varnishes tend to be slightly sticky. Use the information on page 21 to determine your ideal measurements. Make a template of the arm of your machine and transfer it to your chosen surface material. Cut an opening that will fit tightly around the arm of your machine. You'll have an excellent working surface to support your quilt, freeing up your hands for quilting.

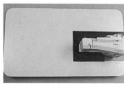

Large extension table

Chairs

Your chair is just as important as your sewing surface. It can make the difference between a pleasant sewing session and the misery of shoulder strain. Your chair should be comfortable and provide firm support. If you do not already own such a chair, prepare for another shopping adventure.

Herman Miller Aeron Chair

SHOPPING FOR THE PERFECT CHAIR

Once again, leave checkbooks and credit cards at home, and try out as many chairs as you can. Shop with the intent of finding the perfect chair for your body, rather than the least-expensive option. I find that women in particular worry more often about what something costs than whether it is the ideal choice. I found that when I shopped by price, I relegated myself to chairs that did not fit properly, and were not constructed well enough to stand up to the long hours I put them through. However, when I shopped based on comfort and fit, I could justify the price.

In short, buy the very best chair you can afford. Often you can find high-quality, inexpensive chairs at railroad salvage or used-office-equipment stores. Government auctions and surplus warehouses offer tremendous values, and don't forget about eBay. Just try not to buy on price alone. At $69.95, that chair may seem like a great deal, but how will it feel after six hours of quilting?

Look for the following important features as you shop:

▣ A center hydraulic-lift system that allows you to adjust the height of the chair. You should be able to adjust the seat so it is low enough for your feet to rest flat on the floor, yet high enough for your forearms and hands to be at the proper angle to the sewing surface and for you to look down on your work as you quilt. Your thighs should be parallel to the floor (at a 90° angle to your body), or nearly so, when you are seated. If you can't find a chair that will adjust to meet all of these requirements, give priority to the position of your arms. You can always use a platform for your feet to make up for any gap.

▣ A seat with a forward-tilt adjustment. This feature takes pressure off the back of your legs, pitches you slightly forward, and keeps your back straighter.

▣ A seat that is proportional to your body size. If you're very small, a small seat will be fine, but if you're larger, it will not provide you with the needed base and support. Seat-test many chairs to feel the difference in comfort level.

▣ A back that is adjustable. Does it pivot or slide in and out? If you need to sit on the edge of the chair or in the center of the seat, can the chair back be adjusted to reach your back and provide the support needed for long periods of quilting?

▣ A base that features five casters or "feet" to insure good balance and stability.

▣ Arms, if you prefer them. If so, you'll want them adjustable so they are not in the way when you don't need them.

Once you've chosen a chair, lift it high enough so that you can look down on the presser foot and fabric. You need to see the needle going in and out of the hole in the presser foot. Relax your arms and hands. Place your hands on the quilt as though you are playing a piano. Lift the wrists, keeping the fingertips on the surface, so the fingers are ready to walk wherever you need them. By positioning your hands in this manner, the stress to your wrists is minimal. If your hands or wrists begin to ache, readjust the height of the chair and the position of your hands.

Lighting

Lighting is another aspect often overlooked in planning a work space. Without proper and sufficient light, you'll be constantly plagued by eye fatigue. Sufficient wattage is the most important issue, regardless of the type of lighting you choose. Overall lighting should be enhanced with task lighting at the machine. Here are some general guidelines for providing sufficient overall light in your workroom.

▣ Eliminate glare. Direct and reflected glare causes eye-strain and discomfort. However, don't over-shield the light source. Provide just enough shading to eliminate glare.

▣ Provide bulbs with adequate—but not excessive—wattage in fixtures and lamps.

▣ Keep colors light on ceilings, walls, floors, and furnishings to enhance both natural and artificial light.

▣ Avoid excessive contrast in amounts of light from one area of a room to another. This can be corrected by adding more general lighting.

▣ Eliminate shadows. If you have a window in your workspace, place the machine to the right of the window. This allows the natural light to fall on the needle area.

When you are quilting at the machine, you'll find that the machine casts its own shadows that can't be overcome by even the most well-lit room. This is where task lighting comes into play. The light on your sewing machine is only fifteen watts. If the light were any brighter, it would also be hotter, causing problems for the machine's circuitry. However, at fifteen watts, it does not give off enough light to see the lines used to mark the quilting patterns, or the seams when ditch quilting. The addition of good lighting around the needle is critical.

I prefer to use OTT-LITEs at my machine. These lamps give non-glare, true-color, full-spectrum light that is very easy on the eyes, as opposed to high-intensity incandescent lamps that create uncomfortable glare and reflection. I place the small portable OTT-LITE in front of the needle, to the right, and in front of the control panel.

I also place a Flex-Arm model behind and to the side of the machine. The tilt of the bulb can be changed, which allows me to adjust the amount of light on the surface. This is really helpful when I am working with contrasting colors. If you haven't tried an OTT-LITE or any of the other true-color, full-spectrum lights, try one. You will certainly see the difference.

Tip

Sometimes the light built into your machine casts a glare off the surface of the presser foot. It can also make it harder for you to see on dark fabrics. If your machine allows it, turn the machine light off to see if your vision doesn't improve.

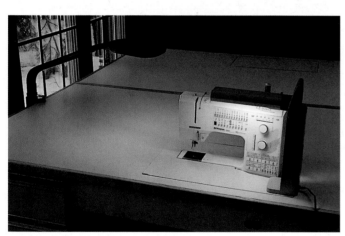

OTT-LITEs surrounding sewing machine

Tip

If your room has windows, and you often work at night, close the blinds or window coverings when it gets dark. You can loose up to 30 percent of the light output in your room from light lost through windows into a dark space.

Tip

Take Care of Your Eyes

Consider wearing reading glasses when you quilt. The slight amount of magnification can really add visual sharpness to the area you are stitching. I have had students tell me they have glasses made for the distance they sit from the machine, so they no longer need to fight bifocals.

Quilting is a very focused activity, and can cause a lot of eyestrain if you don't take steps to address it. Even in the best of environments your eyes will tire. Make it a habit to take frequent breaks and rest your eyes. Every twenty minutes or so, stop the machine, look up, blink, and refocus your eyes on something in the distance. If your eyes feel dry, stop and close them for a minute. Use moisturizing eye drops if needed.

Layering Tables

Students often tell me how much they dislike the job of layering a quilt. My response is that they are not setting up properly. Little wonder sore backs and tucks on the backs of quilts are a problem! Layering on the floor—a method I hear about often—is not the easiest or most successful method. By the time you've gotten everything straightened out and secured on the floor, you wind up crawling on the quilt to reach the center for pinning, causing distortion in the layers right from the start. And —honestly—can you really get up and down from the floor all that easily?

The second most common method I hear for layering is putting two large tables together to make a flat surface the size of the quilt. The obvious problem with this method is controlling the stretch of the backing and reaching the center without back strain.

Mary Ellen Hopkins introduced me to table basting in the early 1980s. Up until this revelation I, too, was on the floor—and much younger than I am now! I've refined this method through the years, and now find layering pain-free, tuck-free—and fast. I work on my cutting table, which is the correct height and width for me (see below).

A cutting table can be one of the most important items in your workspace. You spend as much—if not more—time at the cutting table than at the machine: designing, cutting, planning, marking tops, and layering quilts. This multipurpose table should be customized to your body measurements as well as to meet your space requirements. It should be accessible from all four sides, hard-surfaced, and high enough so you don't need to stoop or bend while working.

Generally, a table 28" to 36" wide x 56" to 72" long is sufficient for layering any size quilt. The narrow width helps eliminate stress on your lower back when you reach farther than arm's length. Ergonomically, your reach should be kept to within 14" to 18" of your body on the table surface. Reaching too far can be awkward and harmful. It also reduces your muscle power. Never stress a joint by over-extending it.

Dual-purpose cutting/layering work surface

Ideally, you should be able to perform the task at hand below elbow level and without stooping. To find the proper height for your standing work surface, stand in the shoes you normally work in, bend an elbow at a 90° angle, have a friend measure from your elbow to the floor, and subtract 2" to 3".

Placing a rubber or padded mat on the floor in front of the table reduces circulation problems and fatigue when you stand for prolonged periods of time. This is especially important if you have a hard floor surface. In addition, wearing flat-soled shoes allows you to maintain good posture. You can also set up a small footstool to rest your foot when you stand for long periods. Alternately rest one foot, and then the other. This helps keep your back straight.

Tip

If you don't have a cutting table, you can substitute a folding banquet table. Raise the height by extending the legs with precut lengths of metal or PVC pipe from the hardware store. (Choose the diameter that will just slip over the legs.) You can also use 4 x 4 lumber, cut the length of the additional height you need, and place under each leg. If you drill a hole the size of the table leg into the top of each 4 x 4, the legs will fit into them securely.

Sewing Machines *and* Accessories

CHAPTER 2

Your Sewing Machine

Your sewing machine is one of the most important tools you own. Think of it as your working partner and your best friend. Sometimes a machine can cause frustration. I often hear students say, "When I get better, I can justify a new machine." Think about this: if your current machine is working against you and causing you frustration, you are not likely to improve. You won't get better until you have a more suitable machine.

Choosing a machine can be overwhelming, especially considering all the machines and features now available, and the price tags attached to them. Too often quilters are sold machines way beyond their needs, or too basic for the work they expect to do. The following list includes features a machine should have to make machine quilting easier.

WHAT TO LOOK FOR IN A SEWING MACHINE FOR QUILTING

- Perfect tension adjustment, no matter what combination of threads you use. It is essential that you can adjust both the bobbin and top tensions.
- Automatic needle stop, so the needle stops instantly when you stop sewing, and does not coast on for one or two more stitches.
- Up-and-down needle position on command. My machine allows me to do this either electronically or with the foot control. One tap of my heel puts the needle down into the fabric, another tap brings it up to the highest position. I don't need to remove my hands from the fabric, which helps me control the quilt.
- A foot control that is not overly sensitive or difficult to control. An overly sensitive control can lead to unexpected sudden changes in speed, which in turn affects stitch length. You should be able to keep the machine at a constant speed without relying on the computerized motor-speed option. The ability to stitch one stitch at a time using the foot control is a real plus when you are quilting difficult patterns, and the machine should be able to sew slowly at a consistent speed.
- A powerful motor to accommodate long sewing sessions. Some quilters want and/or need variable-speed control built into their machine. If you have trouble keeping the machine at a constant speed, regardless of what speed that is, motor-speed control might help improve your stitch quality.
- A needle bar that is clearly visible as you stitch. If you can't sit correctly and see the needle easily, your quilting quality will certainly be affected.
- Adjustable presser-foot height. This feature can be helpful when you are working with different battings and thicknesses. You'll appreciate the ability to raise the presser foot slightly, so the quilt can slide around easier under the foot.
- The ability to sew for hours at high speed without the motor or foot control overheating.
- High-quality feet and accessories made specifically for the machine and for your needs; for example, darning (free-motion) foot, walking foot, straight-stitch throat plate.
- A reputable dealer who will help with minor adjustments, and who understands your technical needs.

Shopping for a Sewing Machine

Begin by finding a reputable dealer and ask for demonstrations on the machines that interest you. Repeat this process for different brands and models. Bring along your own fabric, thread, and batting samples to test on each machine. Ask to take the machine home over a weekend, and then really put it through its paces. It is very difficult to know if the machine suits you when you are watching an in-store demo. We know the salesperson can make it perform, but will it perform for you? Is it easy to understand and program? Does it feel right when you are running it?

When I sold machines, I found that consumers were often intimidated and uncomfortable sewing on the machines in the store. I believe that you need to test drive every machine you are interested in, in the privacy of your home, before making such a large investment. Do not buy a machine based on the recommendation of your best friend or your quilting teacher without trying it first. We all have different needs, and yours may be different.

Keeping Your Machine Clean

Once you have chosen a machine, and before starting the exercises in the upcoming chapters, you'll need to do some preparation. First, clean the machine thoroughly, inside and out. Keep it covered when you are not using it. Dust, lint, pet hair, and various other foreign elements find their way into the machine and can cause all sorts of problems, especially for the circuit boards of computerized machines. Even the smallest particle of lint or debris can cause the machine to skip stitches and have tension problems.

Thoroughly clean the surfaces with rubbing alcohol, and then wax them with a high-quality wax made for the surface material. If your machine has an enameled steel base, use a silicone car wax and buff to a high gloss. (Do not get wax products on the throat plate, as this may cause discoloration.) A product called Quilt Glide makes plastic and acrylic surfaces slick. These cleaning and polishing processes allow the fabric to glide smoothly and quickly through the machine.

Clean between the tension disks on the top of the machine. Fold a piece of muslin in half (or use a pipe cleaner) and rub it between the disks to dislodge any lint or thread fuzz. If you have been using cheap or synthetic threads, dampening the muslin or pipe cleaner with a tiny bit of rubbing alcohol helps clean any residue off the metal disks. You can also use canned air to clean lint from the disks or other parts of the machine. Hold the nozzle about two inches away from any metal parts to allow the propellant to warm before hitting the metal. This prevents condensation on the metal parts of the machine, which in turn can cause pitting of the metal over time. Spray the air from the back to the front of the machine. You don't want to blow the lint into the head of the machine.

Remove the throat-plate cover, and take out the bobbin, bobbin case, and shuttle (hook race) if it is removable. Thoroughly clean the feed dogs. A stiff ½" brush or toothbrush is excellent for cleaning this area of the machine. Brush lint out of every nook and cranny of the bobbin-case assembly, as well as the bobbin case itself. Lint builds up inside the case where the bobbin spins. Every once in a while, slide a coarse piece of thread under the tension clip, and pull out any lint or tiny fibers that may have lodged under it. These fibers can distort the bobbin tension.

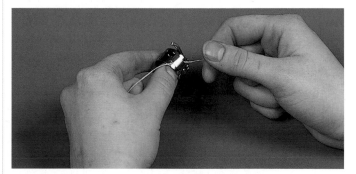

Running a heavy thread under clip to remove lint

Tip

Your computer's tiny vacuum attachment is excellent for sucking lint and loose threads from hard-to-reach places in your sewing machine.

CARE AND FEEDING OF YOUR MACHINE

If your machine suddenly sounds different, stop, clean, and oil it. It generally lets you know when it is "thirsty" for lubrication. Before cleaning and oiling your machine, refer to the manual, or ask your dealer to show you how to clean and oil the machine internally. Lint can pull the lubricants from the metal and cause excessive wearing. Keep the machine well-oiled, but not over-oiled. I recommend that every time you change the bobbin, you clean the shuttle and feed-dog area, and very lightly oil the race, shuttle, and hook areas. There is no such thing as a non-oiling machine! Use a small amount of oil often, rather than a lot of oil once in awhile. Use only the best quality sewing machine oil for your machine. Never use 3-IN-ONE oil or WD-40.

Tips

▣ When opening a machine-oil applicator, do not cut the nozzle tip. Instead, run a large pin down the tip so the oil comes out in tiny drops.

▣ After oiling, rethread the machine and stitch on a fabric scrap until there is no evidence of oil on the thread. You don't want oily thread on your quilt!

▣ Machine-quilter Diane Gaudynski shares this helpful solution for removing oil spots from your quilt: "Sometimes routine oiling of your machine results in a drop of oil on the quilt top itself. Don't panic: blot as much of the oil as possible out with a paper towel, and then take ordinary cornstarch from your kitchen shelf and brush a bit into the oil spot. Use a soft, child's toothbrush so you don't rough up the fabric too much. Let the starch sit on the spot for a day, and then gently brush it away. Most of the oil will be gone, and any residue will be removed when you launder the quilt, or will be absorbed natually into the surrounding areas to become undetectable."

Sewing-Machine Accessories

WALKING FOOT

The walking or even-feed foot is an attachment that allows all three layers of a quilt to move evenly under the foot without shifting or pushing. This foot is a must if you intend to use the feed dogs for machine quilting straight lines (especially long, straight lines) or grids, or for ditch quilting. It fits onto the machine much like a ruffler attachment.

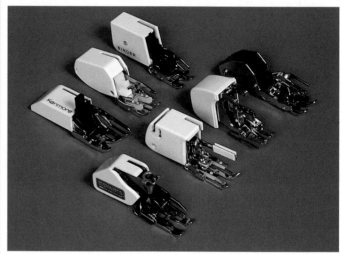

Variety of walking feet

There are actually two "feet" on a walking-foot attachment: the feeders that move back and forth, and the sole plate. As the arm of the walking foot goes up and down with the needle, so does the feeding mechanism of the foot, reproducing the motion of the feed dogs on top of the fabric.

Without a walking foot, the top layer of the quilt is pushed by the presser foot while the feed dogs gather up the backing, causing big problems as you machine quilt. With the walking foot, when the machine forms a stitch, the feed dogs are down and the foot holds the fabric against the throat plate. As the needle comes up, so do the feed dogs. The walking foot lifts the sole plate and sets down the feeders, which line up with the feed dogs. The top and bottom fabric feed evenly, with the feeders lifting and easing in any fullness without tucks or fabric shifting.

Attaching walking-foot arm to needle-clamp screw

Many sewing machine companies offer a walking foot for their machines. For optimal performance, buy the one made especially for your brand of machine. If your machine manufacturer does not make a walking foot, you will need to get a "generic" foot to fit the shank system of your machine. There are several different generic feet available (see the photo on page 28) and you may need to try different ones before you find one that works adequately with your machine. When checking a walking foot for fit, mount it on your machine and lower the presser bar. Make sure the feeders of the foot align exactly with the feed dogs. Otherwise, the pressure does not distribute evenly, and the foot cannot work properly. A poorly fitting walking foot can be worse than no foot at all.

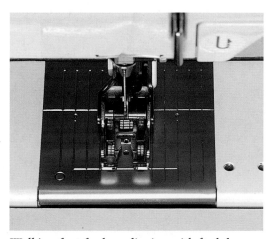

Walking-foot feeders aligning with feed dogs

GUIDE BARS

It is now possible to purchase a walking foot that will accommodate a guide bar for quilting. You'll need a guide bar for each side of the foot, as you may need to guide from either side. These bars "measure" parallel lines for you as you stitch and can be used when you don't want to mark lines.

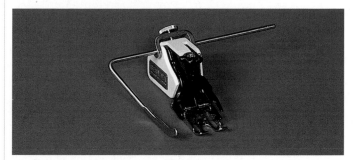

Walking foot with guide bar

SOLVING COMMON PROBLEMS

Typical piecing techniques often create multiple layers of seam allowance in pieced blocks. This bulk causes one of the most common problems encountered when quilting with a walking foot. The foot can get "high centered" on the "lump," cannot pass over it, and stalls. You can either lift the presser foot to release the fabric, making sure that the needle is anchored in the quilt to keep position, or you can make an alteration to the foot itself, preventing this from happening at all.

There are generally three rubber or plastic feeders on the bottom of the foot that align with the feed dogs: two long ones on either side of the foot, and one short one behind the needle opening. It is this short feeder behind the needle that gets caught, as it must pass directly over the seam. By removing the short center feeder, you allow the bulk of the seam to pass under the foot. This does not affect the performance of the foot for normal sewing, but it definitely helps in the quilting process. If the feeders are soft plastic, use an X-ACTO Knife to cut away the feeder. Lay the foot on its side, push the feeders outward, and cut the small, short feeder off even with the sole plate. If the feeders are hard plastic, file them down with a Dremel or similar tool.

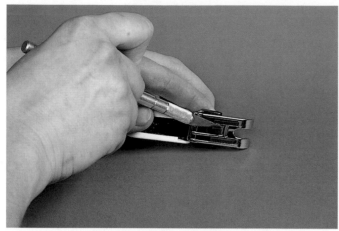

Channel created by removing center feeder

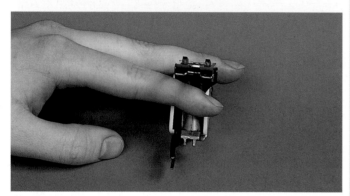

Cutting out short center feeder

Another helpful modification is to open the toes in front of the needle. Use a high-speed cutting or sanding blade on the Dremel tool to cut through the metal to make a wider opening, creating an open-toe walking foot. This allows you to see the ditch more clearly, and is a tremendous help to your accuracy when you ditch quilt.

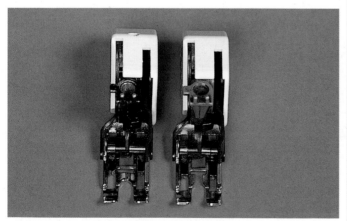

Walking foot before and after opening toes

Too much or not enough pressure on the presser foot can cause uneven stitches. If you can adjust the pressure on your machine's presser foot, you may find making slight adjustments helps the feeding process.

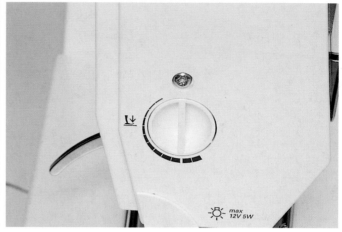

Pressure regulator for presser foot

DARNING FOOT (FREE-MOTION OR EMBROIDERY FOOT)

It is nearly impossible to turn a quilt under the machine to stitch fancy, intricate quilting designs using a regular presser foot or walking foot. A darning foot makes the magic of free-motion quilting possible by allowing you to move the quilt freely under the needle. You must drop or cover the feed dogs when you use a darning foot.

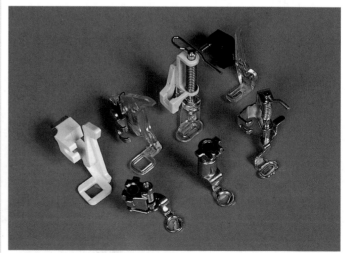

Variety of darning (free-motion) feet

To form a proper stitch, the fabric must be flat against the throat plate as the needle passes through the fabric layers and the throat-plate hole. The clearances for a properly formed stitch are critical. If the fabric is allowed to lift as the needle comes up, a stitch is skipped. The darning foot rises with the needle, allowing "free motion" of the quilt, and then lowers with the needle to hold the fabric down on either side of the needle as it enters the fabric.

If your machine manufacturer does not offer a darning foot, you will need to fit a generic foot to your machine. Be sure the foot lifts properly.

Most generic feet have a spring or bar to the side that rests on top of the needle clamp screw and gives the foot its lifting action. When the needle is in its highest position, the needle clamp screw should lift this bar, which in turn lifts the foot. If the screw doesn't go high enough to lift the bar, the foot won't lift, and there won't be enough space between the bottom of the foot and the throat plate to allow the quilt layers to move. When this happens, you know the foot does not fit your machine.

If you persevere, you eventually will find a darning foot that works for you. Sooner or later you will want a variety of free-motion feet—closed-toe, open-toe, and large—for different applications. No single foot does everything best.

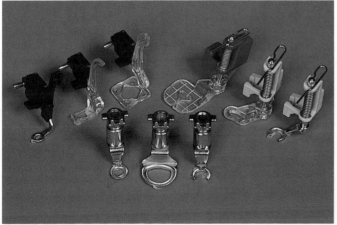

Variety of sizes of darning feet

CLOSED-TOE FOOT

An open-toe darning foot can be problematic when you are quilting larger designs and areas of the quilt. The little toes can get caught in the thread loops formed when you travel across the quilt from stopping to new starting places. The foot also tends to push little bits of fabric ahead of the toes, causing tucks against other quilted lines. A closed-toe foot glides smoothly over the surface, working out any fullness.

Look for a small, round, closed-toe foot that measures $1/4$" or smaller from the needle to each edge of the foot. This is a very useful feature for $1/4$" echo quilting (page 134) and for working the continuous-curve processes (page 128).

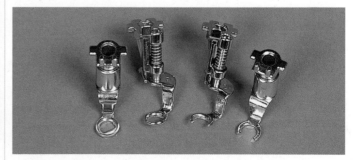

$1/4$" closed and open-toe darning feet

OPEN-TOE FOOT

An open-toe foot is helpful for quilting very small areas and for stitching tiny echo lines or stippling (page 137). The opening allows you to see the exact location of the needle, making it easier to work with than the closed-toe for this type of quilting. Try both and determine for yourself which foot gives you the best results for different techniques.

LARGE QUILTING FOOT

Most better-quality machine companies make a large quilting foot for their machines. This foot is generally square or oval, with a large opening, often marked with printed lines. It is best-suited to quilting thick quilts, such as flannel and wool combinations, or high-loft polyester batting. The foot tends to have a higher stance and more surface area, allowing it to glide over the surface and thickness without dragging, as smaller feet tend to do.

Some larger feet do not sit close enough to the fabric to prevent skipped stitches when you are using a thin batting. If skipped stitches are a repeated problem for you, check the clearance of the foot to the surface of the fabric. Try a different foot to see if the clearances are causing the problem.

Variety of large quilting feet

Tip

When you are quilting a padded (trapunto) design, you'll need a larger quilting foot to accommodate the added thickness of the second layer of batting.

A FOOT FOR EACH PURPOSE

If possible, try to get all three free-motion feet (open-toe, closed-toe, and large quilting foot). You won't know which one you prefer for which situation until you gain experience by quilting sample blocks. Everyone has their own preferences, but what works for each is a personal decision based on experimentation.

THROAT PLATE

The throat plate, often called a needle plate, is the metal piece that surrounds the feed-dog area on the bed of your machine. The standard throat plate on today's machine has an oval opening to accommodate a zigzag stitch. When you quilt, the needle has a tendency to push a bit of fabric into this oval hole, hindering the needle's ability to make a clean, locked stitch. As a result, stitch quality is affected. The bobbin thread sits on the underside, appearing to be "couched" by loops of the top thread, especially when you are free-motion quilting with a darning foot. Sometimes the stitch wobbles and does not look "tight." The larger the opening, the more likely you'll have these stitch-quality issues.

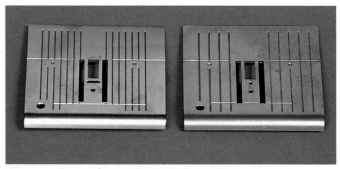

Zigzag and straight-stitch (single-hole) throat plates

A straight-stitch plate opening is too small to allow the fabric to enter with the needle, and therefore helps eliminate puckers and tension problems. This throat plate has a tiny round hole to accommodate only the needle when you are straight stitching.

Make sure the throat-plate hole is smooth, and free of burrs and chips. Often a rough spot is formed when the needle hits the side of the hole. These rough areas can cut and snag the thread as you quilt.

Thread Tension

NOTE: *Read through the entire section on tension before making any changes to your machine. At the end of the chapter, you'll find several suggestions for making samples to test the machine before you start a new project.*

Tension is a mystery to many sewing machine operators. Before changing from one type of fabric or batting, or from project or type of sewing to another, test your stitching on a sample of the new material or project. Inspect the stitch tension and learn to make the appropriate adjustments.

Identify the top-tension adjustment dial on your machine. When doing any type of machine work, make yourself comfortable with the tension adjustments necessary for the machine to stitch properly with the different types and combinations of threads. There is no magic in thread tension, and you can eliminate many service calls if you have a thorough understanding of how tension works.

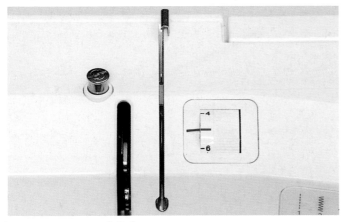

Top-tension control dial

The following exercise will help you learn about tension adjustments. Begin by threading the top of the machine with a 50-weight, 3-ply cotton sewing thread. Be sure the presser foot take-up lever is in the up position. Do not thread the needle. Lower the take-up lever to engage the tension. Position the top-thread tension dial at "normal" and start to pull the thread through the machine. As you pull the thread, lower the tension dial to a lower number, one number at a time. You should notice the thread

getting looser and looser as the numbers get smaller. There should be no drag on the thread when you get to 0. *The lower the number, the looser the tension.* Now go back to the "normal" setting. Pull the thread through again, this time moving the dial up to the higher numbers. The thread will get tighter and tighter, and when you get to 9 or 10, the thread won't budge. *The higher the number, the tighter the tension.*

Sew a row of stitches in two layers of fabric with batting in between. You'll know the tension is correct when both threads are linked in the center of the layered fabrics, as shown in the first illustration below. The next illustration shows the bottom thread being pulled tight, indicating that the top thread is too loose or the bobbin thread is too tight. The third illustration shows the top thread being pulled tight. This indicates the top thread is too tight or the bobbin thread is too loose, a common problem in machine quilting.

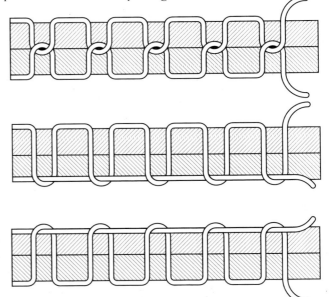

Effects of tension adjustments: (top) - balanced tension; (center) - top tension too loose or bobbin too tight (bottom) - top tension too tight or bobbin too loose

Tip

Make sure the presser-foot lever is down before you start the machine to stitch. It is easy to forget to do this with a darning foot, as the foot does not sit on the fabric when it is lowered. Without the presser bar down, the tension is not engaged.

MAKING ADJUSTMENTS FOR MACHINE QUILTING

The tension adjustments necessary for quilting can be a bit different than for sewing. The layers of the quilt and drag they create, along with the free-motion process, introduce situations for which normal sewing tensions may not fill the bill. When you quilt with matching-size cotton thread in the top and bobbin, and with the properly sized needle (page 48), tension adjustments are minimal, if needed at all. When you use nylon thread in combination with cotton, a combination of different weights of cotton, or silk thread, various tension adjustments may be necessary.

Tip

Often the problem with stitch quality is not the tension, but how you've threaded the machine. Every machine has a specific sequence for threading, and it takes only one missed step in the sequence to cause your machine to skip or produce poor-quality stitches. So often it is the small things that cause the most frustration and lost creative time.

Once you've made a sample of the project and find that corrections are in order, always adjust the top tension first. Many stitch problems can be corrected simply by loosening the top tension. Adjust by one-half number at a time; never make severe adjustments. If the top tension is too loose, loops of top thread form on the bottom of the fabric. If the problem isn't resolved by adjusting the top tension only, then adjust the bobbin tension, seeking a balance to accommodate the project and materials. Tensions can change depending on the type and thickness of the batting, as well as the thread weights and needle size. Test the stitch quality on a sample of the fabrics and batting you'll be using in the actual quilt to determine any necessary adjustments.

BOBBIN TENSION

Be certain you have the correct bobbins for your model and brand of machine. Purchase your bobbins only from your dealer, and make sure they are exactly like the ones that originally came with your machine.

Tension can really be affected by how the bobbin is wound. When winding the bobbin, be sure it is winding smoothly and evenly, and that the thread is being wound tightly. Loose, unevenly wound bobbins cause poor stitch quality.

Poorly wound bobbins compared to a properly wound bobbin

Thread a filled bobbin into the bobbin case. Make sure it is threaded properly. Check your manual to see if the bobbin spins clockwise or counter-clockwise. Most bobbins spin clockwise as you look at them. This allows the thread to come off the top of the bobbin to the right (clockwise), and go back on itself as it enters the slit and passes under the tension clip.

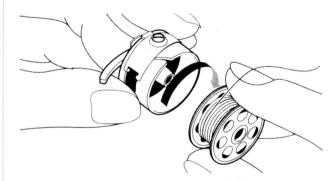

Correct threading of bobbin

Tip

If your stitches are poorly formed, check the threading of the bobbin in the bobbin case. The machine will sew with the bobbin in backward, but it can cause the machine to jam or the stitches to appear crooked on the back side of the quilt.

As a starting point, hold the bobbin case so it hangs freely by the thread. It should not slide down by its own weight, but when you jerk your hand lightly upward, yo-yo style, the case should gently fall. If it doesn't move at all, the tension may be too tight. If it falls easily, it is probably too loose.

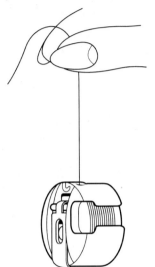

Preliminary test for normal bobbin tension

Before you make any adjustment to the bobbin case, remember to make a note of exactly what you do. I keep a pad of self-stick notes by my machine to record whatever adjustments I make. (This can be a "senior moment" issue for some of us, and it seems the retention rate for bobbin adjustments is "zero.") Draw the diagram below, which resembles a clock face, onto the note. Hold the bobbin case exactly as shown (bobbin on the left, bobbin case upright), and indicate on the note where the screw is positioned before you make any adjustments.

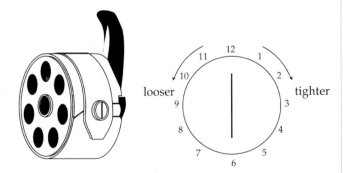

Using "clock face" as a guide for adjusting tension

The large screw on the tension clip adjusts the tension. Turn it to the right to tighten and to the left to loosen. Remember the old saying, *"righty tighty, lefty loosy."* You can adjust this screw in very small increments until the tension is correct. Compare each of your sewn samples to the illustration on page 33. You want your stitches to lock in the middle of the layers, not on the top or bottom of the quilt.

Bobbin tension adjustment screws

Look at the screw as if it were a hand on a clock, and adjust the screw in one-hour (or five minute) increments. Once you have the correct adjustment, draw a new line on your note, indicating where you've moved the screw. Then make a notation to remind yourself where the screw started, and that you turned it to the right to the new "time." When the quilt is finished (with perfect tension!), you can read the note and know exactly how far back to the left to turn the screw. Nothing has been harmed, and the machine is ready to sew normally again.

As an alternative, you can purchase another bobbin case for these adjustments, leaving the original bobbin case set for normal sewing.

Many machines, such as Singer, Janome's, and the newer Husqvarna Vikings don't have a bobbin case. Instead they have a drop-in bobbin housing mechanism. You can generally remove and adjust this unit just like a bobbin case. It has a small screw on the side, and the adjustment is the same as for a bobbin case. Read the screw from the same angle as it sits in the machine. Some machines actually have markings on the housing so you can easily adjust the tension. If you are at all in doubt as to how to make the adjustment on this type of system, ask for guidance from your machine dealer or mechanic.

Bobbin case and drop-in bobbin housing

Tip

With the high speed and long duration of the typical quilting session, bobbin tension can work itself out of adjustment. Knowing how to check and adjust bobbin tension can save you a lot of time and grief. If the tension acts up, stop, clean the machine, change the needle, and adjust the tensions again if necessary.

Tip

Choose a backing fabric for your quilt that is no darker than the lightest fabric in the quilt top. If, in the event of tension problems, a dark bobbin thread appears on the light fabrics of the quilt top, it will always show. However, a light bobbin thread (that matches the light backing) in a dark area of the quilt top can be colored with a permanent-colored marker to act as camouflage.

Keep in mind that different types and weights of thread require different tension adjustments. A bobbin case set for polyester thread may be too loose for cotton thread. Polyester has a high thread drag and requires fairly loose tension, whereas cotton thread has no thread drag and sews better if a tighter tension is applied. Thinner-weight threads slip through the tension clip too freely, while a heavier-weight thread will drag and pull through the same tension setting.

Make it a habit to check the top and bobbin tensions on your machine before beginning each project. Keep a journal of the settings your machine requires for each batting you use, for differences in thread, and needle sizes. All of these factors affect the quality of the stitch. I strongly suggest that a beginning quilter learn how her machine reacts to different circumstances by making samples of quilting using different threads and battings. Experimentation is the best way to learn about tension settings.

TAKING A TEST DRIVE

Always make a couple of sample blocks before you construct all the blocks for the quilt top. As a very experienced quilter, I know that printed pattern instructions are often inaccurate, creating cutting and fitting problems in the quilt assembly. By making sample blocks, you will discover any inaccuracies before you cut and sew a lot of blocks. You can also develop a pressing system that allows all seam allowances to be pressed to suit the quilting later. Once the quilt top is made, and before you layer and start to quilt it, layer these sample blocks with the same batting and backing you plan to use in the quilt.

Thread the machine with the desired threads and do some sample stitching. You will automatically discover if there is too much contrast in the bobbin thread, if the thread has tension issues that will need adjustment, if the batting is difficult to handle, and if the needle is the correct size for the perfect stitch. This may sound like a lot of time and work, but it is certainly easier and less frustrating than ripping out later. Samples are educational and true time savers. They also let you warm up and practice a bit before starting on the real thing.

NOTE: *Occasionally certain machines will snag the nylon thread in the shuttle area. The thread loop does not release off the hook, and the fabric movement is stopped dead. Your only solution is to jerk the fabric to release the thread, and go on. Usually the thread doesn't break, but just leaves a loop of nylon on the bottom of the quilt. This is generally a sign that your mechanic should make a slight adjustment in the machine's timing to accommodate the ultra fineness of nylon.*

Don't be afraid to experiment and play with your machine. It is a wonderful tool with the potential to create anything you can imagine. Take classes and sit in on demonstrations with various dealers of various brands. They know all the tricks you can apply to your machine.

Tips

▣ If you readjust the tensions for a machine-quilting project, don't forget to reset them before sewing again.

▣ Testing for Normal Tension

Here is a trick that my sewing machine mechanic uses to test tension for stitching regular seams. Fold a piece of cotton fabric in half and stitch a line of stitches on the bias. Use a different-color thread in the bobbin and on the top. With your hands about three inches apart, grasp the bias line of stitching, and pull with an even, quick snap until one thread breaks. If the broken thread is the color of the top thread, the upper tension is too tight. If the broken thread is from the bobbin, the upper tension is too loose. To balance the tensions, adjust the upper tension setting on the machine until the threads break at the same time. If it takes quite a bit of force to break both threads, the tensions are balanced.

Threads
and Needles

I f your biggest concern about learning to machine quilt is time, the last thing you need when you sit down to stitch is to have something go awry with your sewing machine. Broken needles, thread jams in the bobbin area, skipped stitches, unsightly thread and stitches, and tension problems are just some of the frustrating issues that can keep you from starting, let alone finishing, a project. Not only are beginners plagued with these problems, experienced quilters have them as well. While your first instinct may be to throw the sewing machine out the window, there are definite reasons machines behave as they do, and this chapter covers the two biggest ones.

Threads

Generally little consideration goes into the purchase of thread, but thread is extremely important to the longevity of a quilt and the performance of your sewing machine.

Buy the highest-quality thread available for all your sewing projects, but be especially careful when purchasing thread for your quilts. Cheap thread is definitely not a bargain! The fibers of poor-quality thread split easily, causing the thread to knot and break as you sew. It also causes a build up of lint in the bobbin area and lower housing of the machine, as well as in the threading system from the spool to the needle. Purchase the highest-quality thread and you'll minimize the potential problems with your machine and tension settings.

Why else should you be concerned with the thread you use in your quilts? The answer has to do with thread strength and fiber compatibility. There are two guidelines to remember when you are deciding on thread for a quilting project:

1. Choose a thread that is weaker than the fabric you plan to use, especially for the construction of the quilt top. I prefer a 3-ply, 100-percent mercerized cotton both for piecing and much of my quilting. Years from now, after your quilt has had much use and many launderings, you will appreciate this choice of thread. If the thread is too strong, it can cut or weaken the fabric in the seam. If a stitch breaks in the seam, it can be mended; if a fabric is cut, it cannot. It is also possible to repair a broken thread in a line of quilting, but it is impossible to repair fabric "cut" by a thread stronger than the fabric. Think of garments you've owned that have ripped when extra stress was put on a seam. Chances are the thread was too strong and abrasive and it wore down the fibers of the fabric in the seam.

2. Threads and fabrics you use in the same project should be of like fibers. For example, natural-fiber fabrics, such as cotton or silk, should be sewn with natural threads; synthetic fabrics with synthetic threads. The only exception is the use of nylon monofilament for quilting. I'll address this in detail later in this chapter.

THREAD SIZING

Throughout this book, I refer to thread sizes in the English-sizing system. The spool states the size of thread as 50/3 or 60/2. There is often an "Ne" in front of the numbers. Be aware that many cone and quilting threads available today have an American-weight system known as Tex. This weight system does not stand for the same thing as Ne, and these threads are not as common. Just remember that if you pick up a spool of YLI, Superior, or Signature thread, (or others acknowledging the Tex system), the number does not mean the same thing as the commonly available threads, and the ply is not always indicated.

COTTON THREAD

I recommend size 50, 3-ply mercerized cotton thread for construction and quilting of medium-weight cotton quilting fabrics. High-quality cotton thread is soft, strong, smooth, lustrous, and resists shrinkage. Check the thread for long, staple fibers; it should not have a fuzzy appearance.

Variety of 50/3 sewing threads

Stitch quality can certainly be affected by the quality of the thread. Slubs in the thread can cause tension irregularities, and fuzzy ends deposit a lot of fiber into the machine. The cast-off fibers absorb lubricants, causing the potential for undue wear on the moving parts in the bobbin area of the machine.

Comparison of four threads of varying quality.
Notice the slubs and fuzziness of the three lower brands.

Some quilters are starting to use 2-ply embroidery threads for piecing and quilting. For years, we have seen evidence that attempts to stitch an accurate ¼" seam allowance don't always work. By using a thinner thread in the seam, you gain back some of the accuracy lost in the stitching and pressing processes. Keep in mind, however, that 2-ply threads are very weak. They generally do not hold up well to the abuse of stress and weight on the seams over time. You can compensate for this by using a shorter stitch length to strengthen the seam, but this makes the stitches harder to rip out if you ever need to do so. My guideline is to set the stitch length so it matches the blade of my smallest seam ripper. As a result, I find stitches made with this thread too small.

Variety of 2-ply cotton embroidery threads

Consider also the distance between quilting lines and shapes when choosing to piece with this thread. If you are doing extremely close quilting, with threads stitched into the quilt closely enough to support the weight sufficiently, or stitched heavily over the seams, it shouldn't be a problem to use 2-ply thread for piecing. Don't use 2-ply embroidery threads if the only quilting you plan to do is ditch quilting, or if quilting distances are spaced further than ½"-1" apart. Avoid pairing 2-ply threads with nylon if you are leaving 1" or more between quilting lines. The nylon is stronger than the embroidery thread, and can cut the weaker cotton. However, if you are quilting with very small stitches, or stitching very heavily (as with tiny stippling), this thread is beautiful and extremely durable.

THREAD SIZES AND THEIR COMMON USES

Thread Size	Uses
50/3 Construction thread	• Use size 75/11 or 80/12 needle • Construction seams for piecing • In bobbin with nylon on top when quilting 1/2" - 1" or further apart • On top and in bobbin when quilting 1/2" - 1" or further apart
40/3 Quilting thread	• Use size 90/14 or 100/16 needle • Construction of heavy weight fabrics • Hand quilting • Machine quilting heavy fabrics • Hand stitching bindings and hanging sleeves
50/2 or 60/2 Embroidery thread	• Use size 60/8, 65/9, or 70/10 needle • Machine piecing with very short stitches • Paper piecing with very short stitches • In top and bobbin for heavy machine quilting 1/2" - 1" or closer • In bobbin with nylon for heavy quilting 1/2" - 1" or closer • Bobbin thread for all forms of machine appliqué • Top thread for satin stitch and straight stitch appliqué • Buttonholes in garments • Machine embroidery
30/2 Embroidery thread	• Use size 70/10, 75/11 or 80/12 needle • Buttonhole and blanket stitch appliqué • Open decorative stitches • Heavy machine quilting
.004 Nylon Monofilament	• Use size 60/8, 65/9, 70/10, or 75/11 needle • Machine quilting • Invisible machine appliqué
10/3 Silk (Clover Tire)	• Use size 90/14 or 100/16 needles – topstitching or embroidery • Hand quilting • Machine quilting
30/2 Silk thread (YLI)	• Use size 65/9, 70/10, or 75/11 needle • Quilting • Embroidery • Topstitching
30/3 Silk thread (Clover Tire)	• Use size 70/10, 75/11, or 80/12 needle • Topstitching • Embellishment • Open machine quilting
50/2 Silk thread (YLI)	• Use size 65/9 or 70/10 needle • All purpose weight • Embroidery • Quilting
50/3 Silk thread (Clover Tire)	• Use size 65/9 or 70/10 needle • Machine quilting • Machine embroidery
100/2 Silk thread (YLI)	• Use 60/8 needle • Appliqué • Very close machine quilting • Fine heirloom sewing
100/3 Silk (Clover Tire)	• Use 60/8 needle • Blind stitch appliqué (hand) • Very tiny machine quilting • All purpose silk thread

SILK THREAD

Diane Gaudynski introduced me to the beauty of silk thread for very fine and close quilting. If you use the same thread in the top and bobbin, there is very little chance for tension problems to occur. (A 60/2 cotton is also a good choice for the bobbin when you are working with silk thread.)

Silk thread comes in different weights: 20, 30, 50, and 100. Size 100 is ultra-fine, and size 20 is the thickest. When you are double-stitching feathers and quilting very tiny stippling, size 100 silk in a 60/8 needle shows no build up on the double-stitched lines. The heavier weights are lovely for single-stitched quilting lines. The only downside is the high cost of silk thread, which could be a deterrent for a larger quilt with extensive quilting.

Various silk threads

CHOOSING A THREAD

As you start to look at the variety of threads available, you will encounter the new, heavier-looking "machine quilting" threads being aggressively marketed to quilt shops. These threads emerged with the evolution of commercial machine quilting and the large, all-over quilt patterns done on longarm quilting machines. The thread is intended to be the focal point on the surface of the quilt. It comes in many variegated colors and is rather stiff on the spool. If you prefer this look, you might like the thread, but when I experimented with it, it couldn't

give me the refined look of heirloom machine quilting that I want on my quilts. When I double-stitched feathers, for example, the thread built up way too much. On the other hand, 50/3 Mettler results in heavy-looking stitches, while retaining the softness of a fine sewing thread and without the tension hassles commercial threads often bring to our home sewing machines. My best advice is to try them to see if they are right for the look you prefer, and for your machine.

NOTE: *Just A Thought*

*The most important thing to consider when presented with a new idea is to think it through **completely**. What is the person suggesting the change doing in her own quilting? If she quilts very heavily, and recommends a very fine thread to piece and quilt with, you know why: it makes for a much finer finished piece. If you don't take that into consideration, and use the suggestion in a quilt that is ditch quilted 5" apart, you are likely to have problems. This explains why there is so much disagreement among quilters in all things technical.*

*When you come upon a new product, learn about its intended true end use. What does the advertising **not** say about the product? **Remember: all things are relative.** Often if we don't consider all aspects of the situation, and—as a result—run into problems, we find fault with the product or technique. This is why I think educating yourself in the technicalities of the craft is essential to the quality and overall enjoyment of any project you undertake. Yes, it takes time to learn about the science of textiles, but the comfort level you experience in everything you do in the future is unequaled. You will no longer jump blindly from one idea to another; you will test and decide for yourself whether or not the "solution" suits your needs.*

INVISIBLE NYLON (MONOFILAMENT) THREAD

Invisible nylon is a continuous nylon filament that comes in a clear or smoke color. The clear thread is designed for use on light-colored fabric and the smoke thread for darker fabrics. Only the depression of the quilting line is visible, not the thread itself. The thread takes on the color of each fabric it crosses, as opposed to regular cotton thread, which is highly visible when crossing many colors of fabric.

Invisible nylon is the only exception I make to using cotton threads in cotton quilts. I am constantly asked why I use nylon in my heirloom-style quilts, and my answer is simple: I am a machine quilter. I do not care for the look of cotton thread stitched over the top of beautiful patchwork or appliqué. Hand quilting leaves those lovely, tiny, up-and-down stitches in the layers. The machine leaves a solid line of thread that looks like a stripe. I think this can detract from the beauty of many quilt tops. When I want the quilting to simply add texture and enhance the piecing, I choose nylon.

Tip

Nylon thread is a good choice for beginning machine quilters. It is very forgiving and encourages the beginner to keep quilting, as any mistakes and uneven stitches are "invisible."

Be very critical of the quality of nylon thread you purchase; there is a vast difference in weights and qualities available. Failure to use the proper thread can result in broken stitches, torn fabric, and undue wear and tear to both the quilt and your sewing machine. The recommendations for brand and size of thread that follow will result in pleasure as you sew, and years of use from your quilts.

Use only the finest, highest-quality nylon threads. These threads are made strictly for artwork, not for sewing draperies and bedspreads. You'll need size .004, and the brand you choose is very important. The most recognized brands are Sew-Art International Invisible

Nylon Thread (my personal favorite) and YLI Wonder Invisible Thread. (Be sure the label says .004.)

You do not want a thread that is coarse or stiff. When testing nylon thread, try to break the thread. It should break fairly easy. If it breaks too easily, it will not hold up to the weight of a quilt. If it is difficult to break, it will cause wearing on the fabric. Don't buy nylon thread that comes on large cones, as the weight can be slightly different from the small tubes, and the thread becomes brittle when stored on the cone for long periods. Buy thread in smaller amounts to keep it fresh.

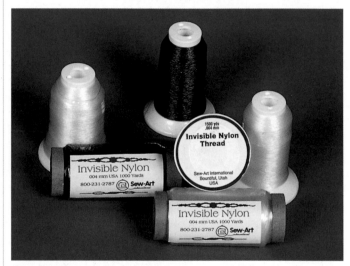

Sew-Art tubes and cones of .004 invisible nylon

Look for thread packaged on 3"-long cardboard tubes or small (about 2$\frac{1}{2}$") white cones as pictured above. The thread should not be wound on a standard thread spool, or jump off the spool like a spring when the package is opened.

When you open the package, run your fingers down a length of the thread. It should feel as smooth and fine as a hair. If it has a gritty or crimped feel, the thread has been overly stretched in the spooling process, and will tend to break and snarl. Return that spool and replace it with one with smooth thread. Often as you approach the end of a spool of nylon, the thread begins to feel rough, take on the shape of the spool, and start to coil. When this happens, throw the spool away and replace it with a fresh one.

The nylon thread needs to be weaker than the bobbin thread. Regular nylon sewing thread is like fishing line and is very difficult to break. It also feels tough and coarse. If you use this thread, and then apply undue stress to the quilt, the thread can tear the fabric and pop the bobbin thread. The soft invisible nylon thread I've recommended, however, stretches with stress and works with the bobbin thread.

Nylon thread is very useful for ditch quilting. It hides the functional stitches in the ditches of the seams where cotton threads invariably show.

Invisible nylon is the only thread that gives machine quilting a look similar to hand quilting, especially when coupled with cotton thread in the bobbin. The softness of the cotton allows the stitch to bend, giving the stitch a "softer" appearance. **Never** use polyester thread in the bobbin when you are using nylon thread. The abrasive polyester fibers will serrate the nylon, causing unsightly broken stitches. Polyester thread also gives a flat, stiff look to the stitches.

Although you can use invisible nylon thread in the bobbin when you use it on top, it tends to leave a stiff, harsh line of stitching rather than the soft, up-and-down look of cotton and nylon used together. It also lends itself to snarling and breaking of the threads. As a result, I prefer to thread only the top of the machine with nylon, and use either a 50-weight, 3-ply or 50-weight, 2-ply 100-percent cotton thread in the bobbin. I make my one exception when I'm quilting from the back to the front to use the backing print as a quilting design. Then I use nylon in the bobbin and cotton in the top of the machine.

If you do choose to use nylon thread in the bobbin, the winding procedure is different than for sewing threads. Do not use the thread guides and tension regulators, as this causes the thread to stretch. Simply use your hand to guide the thread onto the bobbin as you run the machine.

When using nylon in the top of the machine, you will likely need to loosen your machine's top tension to allow for the weight difference of the two threads, and for the high drag and stretchiness of the nylon. Use no larger than a size 80/12 needle with this thread, and only when working with 50/3 cotton in the bobbin. (Use a size 60/8, 65/9, or 70/10 needle when using 60/2 or 50/2 embroidery cotton in the bobbin.) If the needle holes appear too large, change to a smaller needle. Test to sees how small a needle you can use to achieve good quality stitches.

Avoid putting a spool of nylon thread on either the vertical or horizontal spool pin on your machine. Nylon tends to be slick and comes off the ends of the spool easily. Instead, use a cone holder or small jar to hold the spool upright and off the machine.

Cone holders and jar for holding nylon

Built-in thread guide on older-model Bernina

Set the thread holder on the right hand back side of the machine to keep the thread from getting caught in the quilt. If your machine does not have some sort of thread guide to guide the thread at the same angle as the spool pins, tape closed safety pins to the spool-pin base. (See the photo below, points a and b.) As you thread the machine, insert the thread through the small hole of the first safety pin, through the second safety pin, and then through the normal threading procedure. The thread will track from the same direction it would if it were on the spool pin itself.

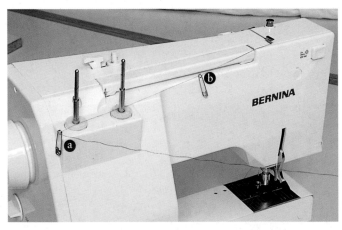

Safety-pin thread guides

Some machines provide a thread guide attachment, or they have one built in. Use this instead of the safety pin if your machine is so equipped, but still use safety pin (b).

You don't need a jar or cone holder for the small white cones of nylon. They simply sit on the table at the back of the machine. Stand them upright so the thread comes off the top.

Nylon thread has a tendency to come off the spool in snarls and loops. These get caught around thread guides and anything else they can attach themselves to. I put a "sock" over nylon thread to keep it gliding smoothly off the spool. The sock is made from a 3"- to 4"-length of $^7/_8$" Surgitube Tubular Gauze (available at pharmacies). It is really for bandaging fingers, but is an excellent aid to control the flow of nylon into the machine.

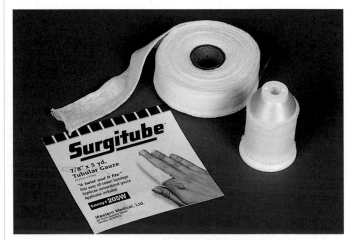

Surgitube gauze used on nylon cones and tubes

NOTE: *Just A Thought*

As I was at the forefront of using nylon in my heirloom-style quilts in the early 1980s, I have probably used nylon longer than almost anyone else. (I've certainly used a great amount of it!) From the beginning, I have used only the Sew-Art International brand. I love the flexibility of this thread, and the fact that it does not shine. All other brands and types of invisible quilting threads tend to shine on the quilt surface, and I find this unacceptable for the type of quilts I make. Sew-Art clear thread takes on the color of the fabric, rendering it truly "invisible."

*Do you run scared by the reports of damage done by nylon thread to machines, fabrics, battings, children, pets, and so on? There are so many amazing rumors that you would think this thread should be outlawed. Keep your logic and common sense in order and remember that nylon is the only way to get the look you want on many of your quilts. Just be extremely careful about **which** nylon you select. I have been using nylon for more than 27 years and have had no problems with broken stitches and damaged fabric, even though my quilts are washed six to eight times a year, travel constantly, and are exposed to severe heat and cold in airplanes monthly. I feel nylon thread has been grossly maligned, and that it offers many more positives than negatives to machine quilting.*

Needles

The sewing-machine needle is probably the number one cause of problems for sewers. It is the first thing to check when you are experiencing stitch problems. High-quality needles are critical to achieving smooth, even quilting stitches. Use the needle type, size, and brand recommended for your machine, and one that complements your choice of thread. Always start each project with a new needle.

Needles are very delicate and easily damaged. Just a slight nick on the shuttle or the throat-plate opening will take the tip off a needle. This can damage the fabric and give poor-quality stitches. A blunt or damaged needle generally makes a thunking or puncturing sound as you sew. Change the needle immediately. Anytime stitch quality changes suddenly, change the needle before making any other adjustments to the machine. A needle that is dull, bent, or simply the wrong size or type can cause major sewing problems. Just because a needle looks good doesn't mean that it *is* good.

> **Tip**
>
> There is no guarantee that all needles in a new package are in perfect condition. A ten percent failure rate per package is not unusual, so you might run across a damaged "new" needle. If you are having problems with stitch quality, don't overlook the needle as a possible culprit, even if it is brand new.

Poor stitch quality can also be caused by needle deflection. This occurs when you use a zigzag throat plate and pull the quilt toward you or to the side when working free-motion. The thread does not stay in the proper position behind the needle because of the pull of the fabric. The hook does not pick up the loop at exactly the right time, creating a sloppy stitch on the back of the quilt. If you consistently get perfect stitches when you guide the quilt away from yourself, but imperfect stitches when you move in other directions, you may be experiencing this problem. You can reduce or remedy it by using a straight-stitch throat plate (page 32).

NEEDLE SIZES

Using the properly sized needle for your project is critical to the quality of the stitch and the well-being of your machine. Needle size must be compatible with the fabric and the thread. An inappropriate needle forces the thread through the fabric, instead of letting it glide cleanly through the needle hole. This can cause broken or sheared threads.

Needle sizes are determined by the width of the needle blade. The European system is widely accepted, but for reference, the U.S. equivalents are shown below.

The information that you need to choose the correct needle is printed on the front of the needle packet. These numbers and letters refer to needle shank shape as well as to length and form of the needle point.

The first set of numbers refer to the needle system. An example is 130/705. The 130 refers to shank length and the 705 indicates that it is a flat shank. These are the numbers that determine which needle system is suitable for your particular machine.

The following letters refer to needle scarf (example: H indicates needle scarf, B indicates no needle scarf). The next letter indicates the type of needle point. (M = sharp, J = Denim, Q = quilting, E = embroidery, and so on) There is often a colored shank to identify needle point type once the needle is removed from the packet.

The needle size is indicated in both metric and US sizes. The metric number represents the needle diameter (size 70/10 = 0.7 mm) This set of numbers determines the needles suitability for a given fabric, thread size, or sewing process.

Tip

The top of the Schmetz needle packet is magnified, making it easier to read the needle sizes imprinted on the needle shank.

Identification labels on needle packages

NEEDLE TYPES

The standard sewing-machine needle is the universal-point needle. The universal needle is a general-purpose needle that can be used on woven fabrics, and was a major breakthrough for sewing on knits. The H stands for *Hohlkehle*, the German word for scarf. This needle is engineered with a long scarf for zigzag stitching. The scarf keeps the needle from hitting or deflecting off the bobbin hook during the formation of a stitch.

Schmetz Microtex Sharp Needle has a thin shaft, and a slim, sharp point that makes very straight stitches. This needle was developed to stitch the fine, tightly woven polyesters and microfiber fabrics that resist penetration with regular needles. Since the point is very fragile, this needle—especially the very small size such as 60/8— needs to be changed more frequently than the universal-point needle. Sharp needles are identified by the purple mark near the shank.

The Schmetz needle company has produced several specialty needles for different sewing techniques and threads. One of these needles is the quilting (H-Q) needle. This needle has a thin, tapered, deep point made especially for piecing and quilting. This new design allows the needle to pass through multiple layers of fabric quickly and smoothly, eliminating skipped and

Needle Size Equivalents									
	Lightweight fabrics				Medium weight fabrics			Heavyweight fabrics	
European	60	65	70	75	80	90	100	110	120
U.S.	8	9	10	11	12	14	16	18	20

uneven stitches. It is excellent for piecing, but the size 75 and 90 are limiting for machine quilting. The size 90 is too large for the majority of threads used for fine machine quilting and is more appropriate for threads such as 40/3, 40 TEX, and heavier, variegated machine-quilting threads. The 75 is too large for embroidery threads and for nylon combined with embroidery-thread weights, but works fine with 50/3 cotton in combination with nylon. If you are experiencing skipped stitches at bulky seams, or tension problems in thicker areas of the quilt, try this specialty needle and see if it clears up the problems. These needles are identified by the green mark near the shank.

The Schmetz embroidery (H-E) needle gives excellent results when you are quilting with rayon threads. The needle has a deep thread groove down the front, a large eye similar to the top-stitching needle, and a special scarf that protects the more fragile embroidery threads. These features guard rayon thread from excess friction during the stitching process, eliminating breakage and weakening of the thread. These needles are identified by the red mark near the shank.

When you are quilting with metallic threads, a Sullivan Metafil needle or the Schmetz Metallica (130/MET) needle is a must. The eye is double-sized and Teflon-coated. The thread groove is deep and the scarf is longer. These needles are designed to eliminate the stripping and splitting of brittle and fragile metallic threads.

If you find that you constantly break the finer-sized needles while quilting, try a 70 Denim (H-J) needle. (The J stands for "jeans.") This needle has a very stiff shaft, a sharp point to pierce tightly woven fabrics, and a slender eye. Be aware that if you have to rip out anything you've stitched with this needle, the holes may remain visible in the fabric.

Quilters often use double needles to create evenly spaced rows of quilting lines. A double needle uses two top threads, but only one bobbin thread, leaving a zigzag thread on the back of the quilt. This may be appropriate for a wall quilt or smaller project, but has the potential of tunnelling, as well as snagging and catching on larger quilts. Experiment with the different spacings available in double needles to test the results.

Tip

When you must change the type and size of needle in your machine, use a tomato pincushion for used needle storage. Mark a different needle size and type in each section of the pincushion. You won't need a magnifying glass to read the numbers on the shank of the needle.

Tomato pincushion for used needle storage

NEEDLE AND THREAD COMPATIBILITY

The following needle/thread compatibility chart tells you the different sizes of needles to use for specific weights of thread. So often difficulties with the machine and problems with stitch quality are caused by the incompatibility of the needle to the thread it must accommodate. Use this chart to determine the best possible combinations.

CHOOSING NEEDLES FOR QUILTING

The most common needles for quilting are universal and sharp-point needles, with specialty needles reserved for decorative threads. Maurine Noble's and Elizabeth Hendrick's book *Machine Quilting with Decorative Threads* (see page 175) is an excellent resource on decorative threads, which are not covered in detail here.

Nothing slows you down more than a broken needle; you tense up just waiting for the next break. For this reason, I recommend that beginners start with a size 80/12 universal (H) or sharp-point (H-M) needle when first learning to machine quilt, especially when first starting to practice. Size 80/12 needles hold up well to abuse, while a smaller, more delicate needle is more subject to breakage until you develop a rhythm with your free-motion work. Use 50-weight, 3-ply cotton thread with an 80/12 needle, either on top and bottom, or in the bobbin with nylon. As you gain more and more control, you'll find that the size 80/12 needle leaves holes in the fabrics, and can sometimes be the problem with bobbin thread showing through to the top, especially when paired with nylon monofilament. It is an especially large needle for quilting with nylon or for ditch quilting. I seldom, if ever, use needles larger than 80/12s.

As you practice and gain more control, switch to a size 75/11 universal (H) or quilting (H-Q) needle; the stitch holes are slightly smaller and the stitching can look more precise. Move on to a 70/10 universal (H) point, and change the thread to 50-weight, 2-ply or 60-weight, 2-ply machine- embroidery thread, both top and bobbin, or in the bobbin with nylon on top. Your stitches will become even more refined.

Next try a 70/10 sharp point (H-M) needle: getting better? You can also experiment with a 65/9, but the ultimate needle is the 60/8 sharp (H-M). This is an extremely thin, delicate needle, and you will be amazed at how fine the quilting stitches look. It is excellent when used in combination with nylon thread on top and 50/2 or 60/2 embroidery cotton in the bobbin; 50/2 or 60/2 embroidery thread in the top and bobbin, and especially for 100-weight silk thread. Your stitches will get smaller and smaller as you decrease the size of your needle. If you want a highly refined look to your stitches, you'll need a very small needle.

Needle/Thread Reference

Thread Size	Needle Size							
	60	65	70	75	80	90	100	110
Ultra fine 80/2	•	•						
Nylon monofilament	•	•	•	•	•			
Fine machine embroidery 60/2	•	•	•	•				
DMC machine embroidery thread 50/2		•	•	•				
Embroidery thread 30/2			•	•	•			
Merc. cotton sewing thread 50/3				•	•			
Synthetic sewing thread (spun)				•	•			
Cotton-wrapped polyester						•		
Cotton 40/3						•	•	
Buttonhole (cordonnet)							•	•

By experimenting this way, you get the best of both worlds. You get trouble-free practice time with a large needle and no fear of breakage, but quickly see great results just by changing thread and needle sizes.

Tip

Choose the thread you want to use before selecting the needle. The needle is determined by the weight and type of the thread.

Remember that all is relative as you decide which thread and needle to use for free-motion quilting. If the quilting pattern has large spaces between the lines and you want the stitches to look heavy, any larger needle with heavier thread will get the job done. However, if you want to create tiny stippling, echo quilting, or do very small shapes, you'll need a finer needle and very fine thread. As always, make samples. They give you an excellent—and sometimes the only—preview of the results of your choices.

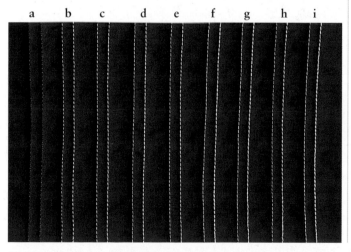

Single and double-stitched lines: a) Sew-Art .004 clear nylon, b) YLI 100 silk, c) Tire 50 silk, d) Mettler 60/2 embroidery cotton, e) DMC 50/2 embroidery cotton, f) Mettler 30/2 embroidery cotton, g) Mettler 50/3 cotton, h) YLI Machine Quilting thread 40 TEX, i) Mettler 40/3 quilting thread;

Needles for Ditch Quilting

An 80/12 or 75/11 needle works perfectly for ditch quilting flannel. The stitches don't show at all. Then you switch to quilting a batik or fine cotton, and the stitches are actually away from the ditch! This is caused by the width of the needle blade. The larger the needle, the wider the blade. If you let the edge of the needle rub the seam, and the needle is wide, you will actually be stitching out from the ditch. Do the ditch quilting with a smaller needle. The blade width is narrower and so the stitches get closer to the actual ditch of the seam. (You can see this when comparing the photos on page 105.) Make sense? Again, try different needles and threads on your sample blocks.

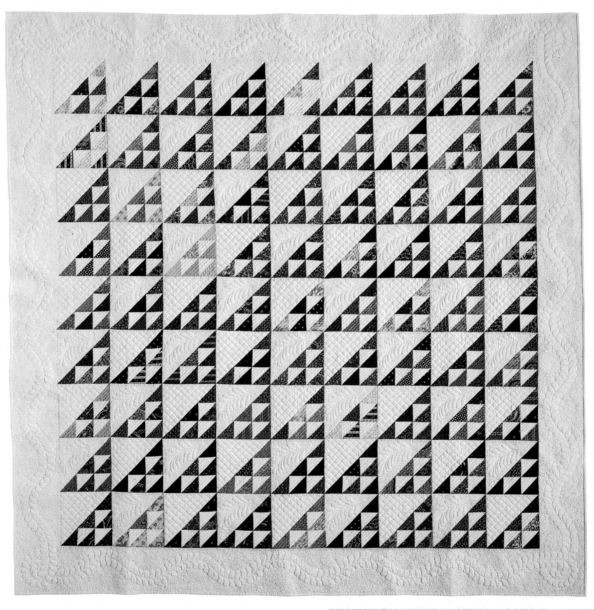

Birds in the Air
78" x 78", Blocks pieced by Jo Morgan, Nashville, TN and quilted by Harriet Hargrave.
This rendition of a circa 1850 quilt features ditch, grid, and channel quilting using a walking foot, as well as free-motion feathers and stippling. Hobbs Heirloom Premium cotton-blend batting; Sew-Art International Invisible Nylon clear thread on top; 50/2 DMC embroidery thread in the bobbin.

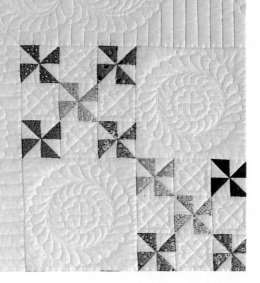

Bridgette's Pinwheels

81" x 95", pieced and quilted by Barbara A. Perrin, Pullman, MI. Pattern from Quilts from the Smithsonian *by Mimi Dietrich.*

Barbara used ditch, channel, and free-motion techniques. This was Barbara's sixth quilt. Fairfield Poly-Fil Extra-Loft batting; YLI Wonder Invisible Nylon thread on top; 50/3 Mettler "Silk Finish" cotton thread in the bobbin.

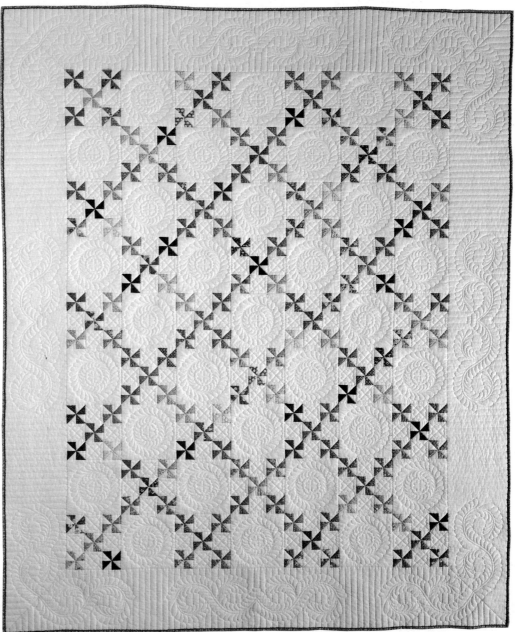

Mary's Currants and Coxcomb
*82" x 82", appliquéd and quilted
by Barbara A. Perrin, Pullman, MI.
Pattern from* Great American Quilts—
1994 *by Nancy Smith.*

Fairfield Poly-Fil Extra-Loft batting; YLI Wonder
Invisible Thread on top; 50/3 Mettler "Silk Finish"
cotton thread in the bobbin.

Sonoma Star

63" x 63", pieced and quilted by
Julie Yaeger Lambert, Erlanger, KY.
California Feathered Star design. Mountain
Mist Blue Ribbon cotton batting; Fairfield
Low-Loft polyester batting for trapunto; 50/3
Mettler "Silk Finish" cotton thread on top and
in the bobbin.

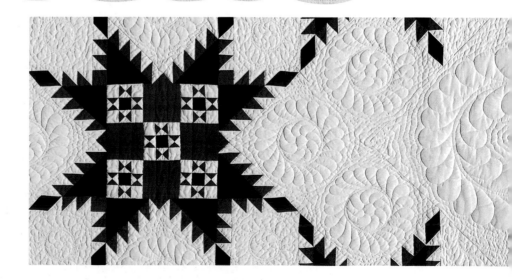

English Strippy
60" x 64", pieced and quilted
by Harriet Hargrave.

Cotton-sateen strips give an authentic look to this quilt, inspired by a style classic to the British Isles. Quilting designs from a late-nineteenth century quilt made in County Durham, England. Hobbs Heirloom Washable Wool batting; 50/2 DMC embroidery thread on top and in the bobbin.

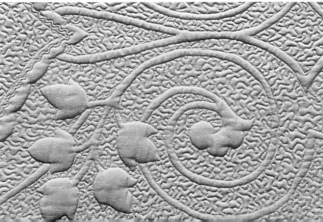

Aqua Table Runner

14" x 34", designed and quilted by Joanie Poole, Sun Prairie, WI.

Joanie used free-motion and stippling techniques. A fancy iron door grate inspired the quilting design for this piece, which is accentuated with trapunto. Quilters Dream Cotton batting; YLI 100-weight silk thread on top and in the bobbin.

Bountiful Vineyard

*35" X 35", designed and quilted
by Joanie Poole, Sun Prairie, WI.*

Heirloom machine-quilted grapes, leaves, and vines
surround a vibrant grapevine wreath. Patchwork wreath
from a pattern featured in *Creative Quilting*, (Jan/Feb
1996; no designer listed) designed for the "I Heard it
Through the Grapevine" fabric line by Quilters Only.
Quilters Dream Cotton batting; YLI 100-weight silk
thread on top and in the bobbin.

PART TWO

PREPARING THE TOP
FOR QUILTING

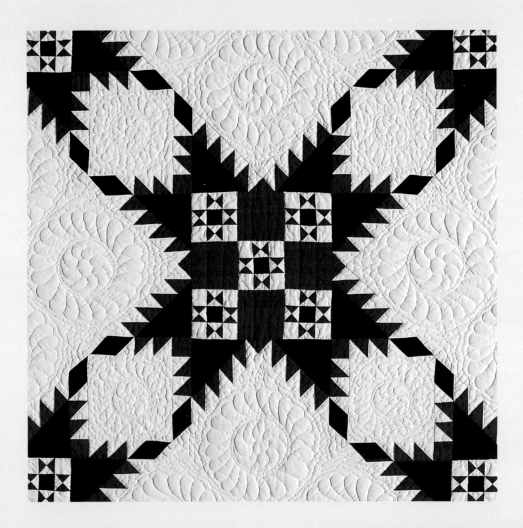

Planning *Ahead*

CHAPTER 4

G reat quilts result from careful planning in both the piecing and the quilting stages. This chapter will help you make decisions about fabric care and construction techniques, as well as basic design ideas that can affect your enjoyment and success with machine quilting. You'll need to consider fabric choice, preparation method, piecing, pressing techniques, and quilting designs, as well as batting choices to create a great quilt. Each interacts directly with the actual quilting.

Before You Begin

There are several general issues to consider when you begin to plan your quilt and the quilting. General considerations appear below, followed by some very specific matters to decide before you even buy fabric for the project. Read though them carefully to prepare yourself for machine quilting that is as trouble-free as possible.

Fabric Choices: Before choosing fabrics for a project, or before planning the quilting designs, consider the level of your quilting skills. Solid and light-colored fabrics, especially muslin, white, cream, and pastels, allow the quilting stitches to be very visible. If you are proud of your skills and want the quilting stitches to really show, these fabrics will showcase them nicely. However, if you still have a ways to go in developing your skills, consider using busy prints and dark colors for the pieced top. This is illustrated by the photo on page 63.

Marking Methods: Think about how you want to mark the quilt top. (Various methods and tools for marking quilting designs onto fabric begin on page 67.) Machine quilting requires a very visible line. Dark colors and busy prints can be very difficult to mark, and the lines hard to see. If you want to quilt feathers and detailed designs, your fabric choice will not only affect marking, but the visual effect you'll get when the quilting is finished. Quilting tends to disappear into busy prints.

Thread Color: Think about the thread color you want to use on the top for quilting. Skill level is again a consideration here. If you want your stitches to be visible and/or decorative, a heavier-colored thread will show on the surface. However, if you want to disguise your mistakes, consider a thread that matches or totally blends into the fabric—or use nylon. Nylon is a perfect choice if the quilting lines cross over different fabrics and colors. If you'd rather not use nylon, and aren't concerned about time, you can change thread color to match each fabric.

Quilting Density: The amount of quilting should be consistent and evenly spaced over the entire quilt to prevent distortion. Contraction, the natural shrinkage that occurs when the layers are stitched together, plays a big part in the final look of a quilt. The more heavily you quilt an area, the more contraction you'll get.

Batting: Batting is a major factor in the look and success of the finished quilt. The style of the quilt, the amount of quilting you desire, the texture you expect from shrinkage, the thickness and/or softness you want after quilting, the size and difficulty in handling the quilt under the machine—all are affected by the batting you choose. A poor choice of batting can create major stumbling blocks in the quilting process.

FABRIC PREPARATION: TO PREWASH OR NOT?

Fabric preparation begins when you choose fabric for your quilt and affects how you care for it from that moment on. Should you prewash the fabrics or not? What are the advantages and disadvantages of both? Have you really looked at the options to find which way you prefer to work with the fabrics? You might try making a quilt with prewashed fabric, and another with new, unwashed fabrics to see for yourself.

There is no *one* right way to do anything. How you treat your fabric is relative to the look you want for the final product. A number of years ago, I wrote a book titled *From Fiber to Fabric* (see page 175) to provide quiltmakers with a textile reference that detailed the textiles we use for making our quilts: fabric, thread, and batting. Because I have worked with manufacturers of batting and fabric for so long, I have excellent resources and people to rely on for accurate answers to the problems we experience with our fabrics.

Instead of telling you to do things the way I do because it is the right and only way, I believe it is my job as a teacher to show you how to test your fabrics to find the answers for yourself. I do not prewash my fabrics, as I desire the slightly puckered look of antique quilts in my finished quilts. Not everyone wants this look, so it is not the choice they make. If I prewashed my fabrics, I would not be happy with the end result, so I consider this my decision to make based on testing different options to come to a conclusion. If you don't take time to learn the various possibilities, how can you make an informed decision?

Why do I even bring this up? When you work with a sewing machine, you must consider the needs of the machine. Sewing machines benefit from crisp, firm fabrics in order to sew accurately. Prewashed fabrics, especially with today's soft finishes, can become very soft and limp. This has the potential to cause problems with piecing, and distortion with cutting and pressing. The fabrics may become overstretched when layered, and form tucks and puckers during the machine-quilting process.

I have always believed that the prewashing "rule" was established by hand piecers and hand quilters, as they prefer to work with the softer feel of the fabric. Dressmakers have also contributed to the theory of prewashing, due to shrinkage issues in garment construction. However, the machine is such a big part of what we machine piecers and quilters do, I prefer to cater to *the needs of the machine*, making it easier to work with.

Start thinking about the finished look you want for the quilt before you do anything to your fabric. I encourage you to experiment with samples, trying different methods of fabric care. Choose what works for you and gives results to suit your taste.

The bottom line is this: preparing the quilt top for quilting begins with the piecing. Whether you choose to prewash your fabrics or not, the reality is that a crisp finish makes it easier to cut and sew the fabrics, and plays a big role in making the quilting easier. So…we turn to starch. Starching your fabrics can make the difference between frustrating and fantastic! If you prewash your fabrics, starch restores the crisp finish. If you do not prewash, the starch assures that the seams are flat and crisp. Either way, *starch is magic for machine piecing and machine quilting.*

STARCHING

There are several types of starch to choose from. I personally prefer the dry-powder starch that comes in a box. Three to four tablespoons mixed with a quart of cold water and placed in a spray bottle makes it the most inexpensive option. Since it is less refined than the spray products, it gives the most stiffening power of all commercial starch products.

You can also use liquid concentrate starch or spray starch. Follow the product instructions to mix a starch with a medium to heavy finish.

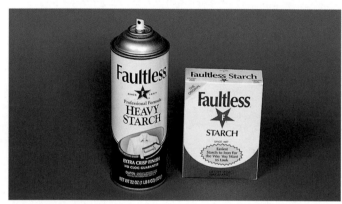

Spray and dry starch

Protect your ironing board cover with a large piece of muslin. Remove and wash the muslin when it gets too stiff or unsightly from excess starch.

Use a dry iron on the cotton setting to starch your fabric. Spray a light mist over a single thickness of fabric and press. If you have prewashed the fabric, you may need to repeat this process two or three times on each side of the fabric. Don't saturate the fabric, but spray a fine mist instead; you are aiming for a gradual buildup of starch. If starch builds up on the soleplate of your iron, run the hot iron over a damp towel to remove the starch. If it is scorched on, white vinegar can help remove it.

Do not starch your fabrics before storing them. Starch is derived from corn, which is food for insects. If you prefer not to store your fabrics without washing them first, go ahead and prewash, but don't press them. Starch and press the fabrics when you are ready to use them. Always starch the backing fabric until fairly crisp before layering, and press any joining seam allowances open. I use a $1/2$" seam allowance and a slightly shorter stitch when seaming backing pieces together.

Not only does starching the fabrics make cutting easier, but it allows your machine to stitch more evenly, and without "eating" the points of triangles and diamonds. Starched pieces enable you to match intersecting seams more precisely, and to produce more accurately sized blocks, sashing, and borders. Starching also allows you to press seams crisply, and gives you a smoother surface to mark for quilting and a firmer fabric to quilt. Starched fabrics are less likely to stretch or contract during the quilting process, minimizing distortion.

PRESSING SEAM ALLOWANCES

The decision to press seams open or to one side also depends on the type of quilting you plan for the quilt. If you plan to do any ditch quilting, you must have a ditch. Ditches are created when the seams are pressed to one side or the other.

However, if you are making a block with many seams that cross, and you don't plan to ditch quilt any of the seams within the block, you may press those seams open to eliminate bulk at the intersections. Open seams make for a smoother and flatter quilt top, so quilting over the seams is much easier for the machine.

As you piece the blocks of your quilt top, continue the starching process. Sew two pieces together, set the seam, press, lightly starch, and press again. (When piecing, spray only the right side of the fabric.) Continue in this manner until you have completed each block. You'll be amazed at how square and flat your blocks will be—probably more than any others you've pieced before. In addition, the use of starch throughout the piecing process makes the quilt top more secure, preparing it for marking and layering.

NOTE: *If you are new to quilting, or if piecing and pressing are troublesome for you, I recommend that you read Chapter Four of* The Art of Classic Quiltmaking *(see page 175), which I co-authored with Sharyn Craig. It includes detailed instruction in the finer points of pressing.*

PREPARING BORDERS

Consider cutting border strips wider than the desired finished width, and starch them both before and after attaching them to the quilt top. Mark the finished width on each border with a washout marker, so you know where to stop the marked design. Once the borders are quilted, you will be able to trim them more easily and accurately. Measure the desired border width from the border seam, and cut the border parallel to that seam.

I cannot stress enough how important it is to consider the machine quilting process before constructing the quilt top. I constantly encounter students who struggle with tucks, puckers, stretching, and distortion in their quilt tops and finished quilts, all due to lack of preparation to accommodate the quilting process. Quiltmaking is one big package deal, and if you leave out a step or two in the process, you will know it in the end. Take your time, take machine quilting into consideration every step of the way, and you will surely reap the benefits of your efforts.

Choosing Designs to Quilt

I thought about making this chapter the first one in the book, as it covers such an important consideration, even before you begin to piece the quilt top. Thinking through the entire quilt, instead of just the quilt top, is something that beginning quilters are seldom taught to do. Rather than viewing the quilting as just something to hold the layers together, think of how it can complement and enhance the quilt top and give depth to the overall appearance of the quilt. Great quilts come from considering the piecing *and* the quilting in the planning stages.

Today's quilter is inundated with ideas for pattern, design, and color for quilts. Books are filled with wonderful photographs of beautiful quilts, all focusing on pattern, design, and color. But where is the quilting? How often is the quilting not even visible in the photos— if there is even much quilting at all? How often is the quilt quilted with generic meandering on a longarm machine, so the quilting plays no part in the overall quilt design? When you reach the end of a pattern or project, expecting to find ideas for finishing the quilt top, how often do you read "quilt as desired?"

How often are quilt shop samples left unquilted? A growing percentage of quilts at quilt shows are not quilted by the person who made the top. Many are quilted similarly, on commercial longarm machines. Where is our guide and inspiration for quilting all of the tops we've been lured into making based on pattern, design, and color? So often, out of frustration, we neatly fold the top, and start another pretty project, concerned only about pattern, design, and color.

Because I teach quilting and finishing—not design— I find this very frustrating. What happened to turning beginners into quiltmakers, not topmakers? The question I am asked most frequently is, "How should I quilt this?" The problem is, I don't know: it is not my quilt top! We get so wrapped up in seeing the fabrics and patterns emerge that we lose sight of the quilting and what it offers. To complicate the issue, a common belief holds that quilting is difficult, and not as much fun as making the quilt top. I believe that a *quilt isn't a quilt until its quilted* and *the quilting is what breathes life into the top and makes it complete.* I tell my students that my least favorite part of making a quilt is piecing the top. They look at me like I'm crazy. But my favorite part is the quilting—seeing it all come together. If you haven't quilted much or well, you probably like piecing the best. But I know many, *many* quilters who have mastered the quilting and, as a result, think quilting is truly the most exciting part of the process. If you haven't done it, how do you know it won't be your favorite, too?

Quilting Considerations

The more you get involved in finishing your tops, the more you'll start to plan the quilt top around space that shows off quilting. Begin thinking about quilting designs from the moment you start to plan your quilt top and choose fabrics. Visualize the finished project, either on the bed, on the wall, or wrapped around someone special, with the quilting just as important as the piecing and appliqué.

Consider the following when you're in the planning stages of designing a quilt:

◘ Include areas of "white space" in the design. These blank areas show off the quilting and give the viewer's eye a place to rest.

◘ Plan the size of sashing and borders around a specific quilting design. In fact, choose the quilting designs you want to work with, then plan the *entire* quilt around these designs.

As you venture into the world of planning for quilting, ask yourself the following:

◘ Is the quilt designed to be traditional, contemporary, or a reproduction? Is it a specific technique such as bargello, watercolor, Baltimore album, or Amish? The quilting designs you choose should be compatible with the style of your quilt.

◘ What is the purpose of the quilt? How will it be used? Will it get a lot of wear and tear, or is it purely decorative? Will it be laundered often?

◘ How much time do you have or want to spend on the quilting? This is a definite factor in planning the quilting design. If you don't have much time, keep it simple, but if you have made a masterpiece, don't skimp on the quilting.

◘ Is the top made from busy fabrics that will hide the quilting? Are there spaces that would really show off exciting quilting motifs?

◘ What batting will you use? Always take into consideration each manufacturer's recommendations for distance between quilting lines by type and brand of batting. You'll want balance and equal density of quilting throughout the quilt.

◘ Are your technical skills up to the job of transforming your quilting ideas into reality? Consider your level of quilting skill before you begin designing the quilt top. If you are new to machine quilting, think about piecing with busy fabrics to camouflage the stitch irregularities that naturally occur while you are learning to quilt. You can quilt all kinds of patterns on busy fabrics, and you won't be able to see the mistakes easily. (Think of how many quilts you can get done, as well as how much practice time you'll put into your quilting skills—all at the same time.) Solid and sateen fabrics are wonderful for showing off feathers, but if you can't quite stay on the lines, a small print helps to hide the goofs.

Stitches show on solid fabric, not on print.

In summary, think through and plan the quilting at the design stage of the quilt to make wise, thoughtful decisions from the beginning.

Quilting Techniques

The technique you choose for quilting will directly determine the design or look of the quilt. Here is an overview of basic machine-quilting techniques and how they affect your choice of the actual quilting design.

FOUNDATION DITCH QUILTING

One of the most functional forms of machine quilting, and one of the easiest to learn, is ditch quilting. This machine-guided technique is extremely useful for securing the quilt layers together at the start of the quilting process. I use ditch quilting as a method of stabilization above and beyond pin-basting.

Analyze your quilt. Look at the seams that join the blocks and/or the seams that attach blocks to sashing. These seams are perfect candidates for ditch quilting. The stitching won't show, but the ditch quilting will stabilize the layers. Once the ditch quilting is done, you can remove many of the pins, making it much easier to maneuver around the marked designs.

Don't overlook the simple option of quilting the entire quilt in-the-ditch. Ditch quilting is highly functional and many quilts are made with fabrics that wouldn't let the quilting show at all, so this can be a very appropriate and easy solution. For detailed information about ditch quilting, see pages 104-110.

Tip

As you become more experienced with free-motion techniques, you might choose to do your ditch quilting free-motion. Although you are doing all the work manually, there is no chance of distortion with free-motion quilting. This is an excellent way to do short seams in the ditch, or to go around appliqué or pieced shapes that would normally require you to turn the quilt if you were using a walking foot.

GRID QUILTING

Another form of quilting to consider is all-over grid quilting. This machine-guided technique imposes a grid, or one-directional lines, over the entire surface of the quilt, not just around pieced or appliquéd designs. It is a classic way to introduce lots of quilting without the degree of skill needed for free-motion work. Grid quilting can be extremely effective on many different types of designs. For detailed information about grid quilting, see pages 111-116.

FREE-MOTION DESIGNS

When you first begin to free-motion machine quilt, you'll probably find that staying on a marked design line is easier said than done. Free-motion techniques are presented in detail on pages 117-142, but there are some basic guidelines to consider when planning the designs to quilt on your first projects.

Beginners often think that large, open designs are the easiest to quilt: less quilting to fill more space. Just the opposite is true. Smaller, tighter designs (6" or smaller) tend to be easier to quilt, and therefore more successful choices for beginners. The longer and straighter the line, the more you must control and move the fabric. If the lines are short and constantly changing direction, it is easier to move the fabric with your fingertips.

You may want to avoid straight-line designs, or those with lines parallel to one another, especially at first. Your eye will quickly notice quilted lines that are not straight; they become even more noticeable when they are not parallel.

Poorly quilted parallel lines   *Parallel lines quilted accurately*

CONTINUOUS-LINE DESIGNS

If you are new to machine quilting, take care in your choice of quilting designs. If the pattern has separate units or frequent stops and starts, machine quilting will become tedious and time consuming, and the quality of the piece can be affected by many lock offs (page 122) within a small area. Too many lock offs leave a sloppy-looking back, and the potential for thread tails to come loose and stitches to pull out. The designs below are not easily adapted to machine quilting.

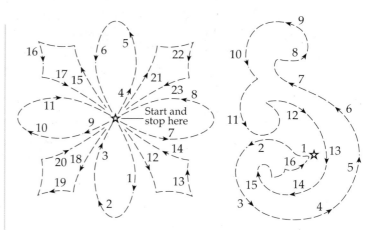

Continuous-line quilting designs

Many designs are not continuous, but often you can find a way to adapt them. Finger-trace the designs below to see how the non-continuous lines can be done on the machine.

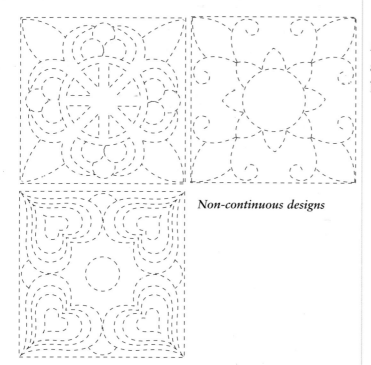

Non-continuous designs

Continuous-line patterns lend themselves perfectly to machine quilting. The patterns can be simple or complicated, but without lines that start and stop or weave in and out. Look for patterns that you can trace with your finger with few—if any—interruptions in the design. Finger-trace the designs below, starting in one spot and tracing the entire design without stopping or retracing any lines.

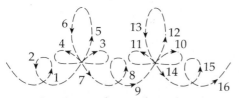

Continuous-line quilting design

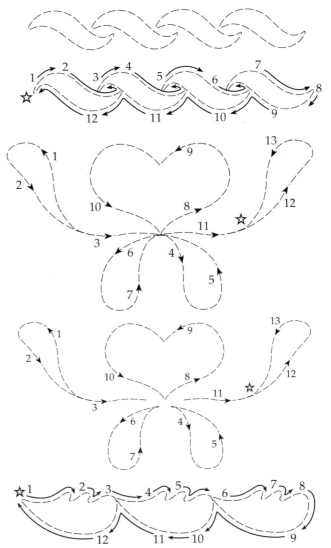

Making non-continuous designs continuous

Before settling on a design for your quilt, work out the order in which it will be stitched. Trace it onto the quilt in the same order that you will stitch it. This trains your eyes and hands to the motion of the design, making it easier to achieve when you are quilting. If you find the design confusing and you get lost easily, it will be even more frustrating when you are trying to control a large quilt at the same time.

Tip

As you learn and practice the various techniques for machine quilting, quilt some full-size block samples of ideas you are considering for a specific quilt. You might include a block design with different background fills, a border section, a sashing strip, or large side-setting triangles. It is often easier to make a final decision when you actually see the quilting on the fabric, sandwiched with batting. You'll also discover if the idea is too time consuming, or if your skills aren't yet up to the task. On top of those benefits, you'll be practicing!

Follow arrows and numbers for order of stitching. Begin at the star.

Stencils, Marking Techniques, *and* Markers

CHAPTER 6

🔲 **NOTE:** *Be sure to read pages 58-66 before proceeding.*

Once the quilt top is complete, press it extremely well. Generally this involves pressing on the right side of the fabric. Once the quilt top is pressed smooth and flat, you are ready to mark the quilting patterns or lines onto its surface. If you are ditch quilting only, no marking is necessary.

Stencils

Plastic, precut quilting stencils are convenient and widely available. They come in a seemingly infinite number of sizes and designs, including many for continuous-line machine quilting. But not every option you wish may be available precut. Often the design is available, but not in the size you need. Here are some tricks for making your own stencils in any size. They are very simple to make, inexpensive, and provide a wealth of options from which to draw.

MAKING YOUR OWN STENCILS

Reduce or enlarge the pattern to the size you want. Most copy shops have equipment that can enlarge or reduce a pattern to any size without causing distortion. Once the pattern is the desired size, there are two ways to make stencils. Both methods give durable, long-lasting results.

To speed your marking time, preplan the cuts so you get the longest line possible. You can cut long straight or wavy lines up to 2½" before allowing for a "bridge," the connection that keeps the stencil from falling apart. Smaller areas and circles must have cuts no longer than ½" to 1" between bridges. Leave a sufficient number of bridges to keep the stencil sturdy and intact.

USING A DOUBLE-BLADED KNIFE

This method is best for designs with long, curvy lines, rather than for small, intricate patterns. You'll need DBK Stencil Plastic for the stencil. This very soft, see-thru plastic, available at many quilt shops, is easily cut with the double-bladed stencil knife made by Olfa. The knife cuts two parallel lines, ⅛" apart.

1. Trace the pattern lines onto the plastic with a permanent marker.

Drawing design lines onto DBK plastic

2. Use a double-bladed knife to cut the channels needed for the stencil. Cut on either a rotary-cutting mat or on a piece of glass. As you cut, lift the knife every so often to create a bridge.

Cutting channel in plastic with double-bladed knife

3. After all the design lines are cut, use a single-bladed knife or a small pair of scissors to clip out the ends of each channel.

4. Wipe off any permanent marker left on the plastic to avoid transferring ink to your fabric.

USING A STENCIL-BURNING TOOL

Another method for making stencils is to use a stencil-burning tool, commonly called a hot pen. This instrument is similar to a wood-burning tool, and is very helpful for making small, intricate patterns.

1. Plug in the pen. While it is heating up, trace your design onto a sheet of Mylar with a permanent pen.

2. Curl the Mylar up and off the surface of the table to achieve a clean cut. Rest your forearm against the table to steady your hand. Insert the tip of the hot pen into the Mylar at the beginning of a design line. Slowly and evenly follow the line with the hot tip. Move along the line, using an in-and-out motion with the tip to keep the cut clean.

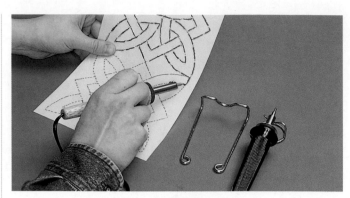

Cutting channels in Mylar with a stencil burner

3. When you stop for a bridge, pull the pen tip straight out, leave a space, and then continue cutting.

4. After the cuts are made, remove the bumps on the back of the stencil with a sanding block or a single-edge razor blade.

Marking with Tulle or Mesh

Tulle (bridal illusion) is a simple, practical option for transferring a design onto the quilt top. Tulle is a very fine, soft netting used to make wedding veils, and is readily available at fabric stores. Mesh is also made for transferring designs.

This method is especially useful for light fabrics that can be marked with a water-soluble marker (page 76). Be aware, however, that water-soluble marking tools don't always show on dark fabrics, dry pencils tend to tear the tulle, and chalk powders brush off too easily.

1. Pin the tulle on top of the design. Trace the design onto the tulle using a permanent black felt-tip marker such as a Sharpie or laundry marker.

2. Wash the tulle in soapy water, rinse, and press with a warm iron to dry. This prevents residue from the marker transferring to the quilt when you mark the quilt top.

Tracing pattern onto tulle or mesh

3. Position and pin the tulle on the quilt top, and use a liquid fabric marker, such as a water-soluble Dritz Mark-B-Gone to transfer your pattern. As you trace the lines, the liquid ink goes into the holes of the tulle and leaves dots on your quilt top to mark the quilting line. When the tulle is removed, the entire design is on the top, ready to quilt.

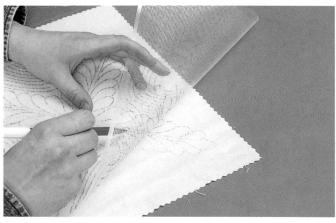

Tracing design lines onto fabric through tulle

Water-Soluble and Tear-Away Methods

Yet another method of marking quilting designs is to use a wash-away product such as Solvy (made by Sulky) or a tear-away product such as Quilt-and-Tear on a Roll paper. These materials are very soft, and either dissolve in water, or tear cleanly away from the stitching. Any residue left in the stitches dissolves in cool water. This method is good for marking dark, busy prints and problem fabrics such as velvet, lamé, satin, sateen, and silk.

This is not a speed technique, but rather a safe method that protects fragile fabrics and allows you to quilt dark, busy prints easily. Several companies now have quilt-and-sew paper available with pre-printed quilting designs.

1. Mark your pattern onto the water-soluble product or tear-away paper with a blue felt-tip, water-soluble marker. The blue lines wash out with water the same as the residue from the paper or other product. For more on these markers, see page 76.

2. Position the tear-away or paper product over the quilt top when layering and basting so the quilt sandwich includes four layers. Stitch directly through the paper on the drawn lines.

3. After quilting, follow the manufacturer's instructions to gently remove the product from the stitching.

Quilting through paper, and then tearing it off

Tracing with a Lightbox

Another alternative to stencils is to use a lightbox for tracing. This method is especially useful for large projects that would require considerable preparation time for stencils or that involve very detailed quilting patterns. I use my lightbox for a multitude of tasks in all phases of quiltmaking.

You can create an inexpensive lightbox with a lamp and an expanding table. Open the table and cover the open area with a sheet of glass. Place a lamp (without its shade) on the floor below the glass. Higher-wattage bulbs make it easier to trace onto dark fabrics.

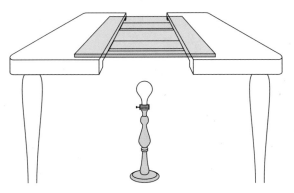

Using a table to make a lightbox

You can also build a wooden box with an acrylic top. Place kitchen under-counter fluorescent light sticks in the box. Ready-made alternatives include a child's Lite-Brite toy or the small inexpensive lightboxes available at quilt shops and craft stores.

You may be able to adapt your sewing-machine cabinet for use as a lightbox. Remove the machine from the cabinet and place a fluorescent light on the surface where the machine usually sits. Have a thick piece of Plexiglas cut to fit the opening. This gives you an excellent lightbox surface.

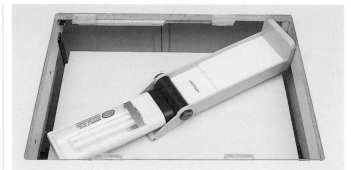

Using a fluorescent light in your sewing-machine cabinet

1. Use a bold black pen or marker to trace the quilting pattern onto white butcher or freezer paper.

2. Tape the pattern onto the surface of the lightbox. Turn on the light, allowing it to shine through the surface and the paper.

3. Position the quilt top over the paper. Even black fabric becomes translucent, enabling you to see through the fabric to the marked lines. Trace the lines onto the quilt top, repositioning it as necessary.

Using a lightbox to trace designs onto fabrics

Pin-Prick Method

Antique quilts are excellent sources for quilting designs, including originals not found elsewhere. To copy a pattern from an antique quilt, place a sheet of brown craft paper or freezer paper over cardboard, a sheet of cork, or a piece of carpeting. Lay the antique quilt on top of the paper. Insert a very fine, sharp pin or needle through the quilt to pierce holes in the paper as you follow the quilting lines. This method of transferring the pattern does no damage to the quilt and eliminates the risk of making lines on the quilt by surface tracing. It also eliminates excessive handling of a delicate textile.

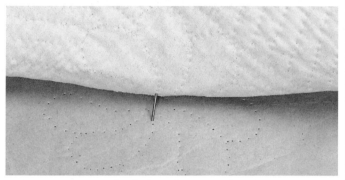

Using a pin to transfer designs from a quilt onto paper

Preparing the Quilt for Marking

Before transferring any designs onto the quilt's surface, you must mark registration lines for accurate placement. Precut stencils are not always perfectly aligned on the plastic, so you must determine the actual size of the design and how it should sit on the quilt. The measurement you need is the actual area of the design itself, not the plastic.

BLOCK OR FILL DESIGNS

For block stencils, find the exact center of the pattern, as well as the center points on the outside edges of the design. Mark these registration lines onto the stencil with a permanent fine-line marker. Measure the quilt block to find both its center point, and the midpoint on each outside edge, and identify with a water-soluble marker. Align the registration lines on the stencil with the key markings on the block. This assures a well-centered design.

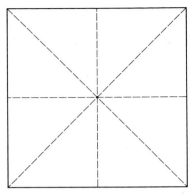

Registration lines for quilt block

Registration lines for stencil

BORDERS AND CORNERS

Follow these instructions to establish registration lines on borders and corners.

1. Mark a 45° angle line in each corner of the border.

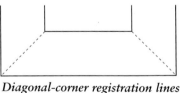

Diagonal-corner registration lines

2. Use a ruler to draw a line that extends the border seamlines across the width of the border on all sides.

Corner registration lines

NOTE: *If you have cut your borders wide to accommodate trimming, you will need to determine the finished width now.*

3. Measure from the border seam to the edge of the border. Subtract the ¼" outside seam allowance from this measurement and determine the midpoint of the border width. Measure out from the border seam and mark a dot at each corner on the lines drawn in Step 2. Connect the midpoints with a line the length of each border.

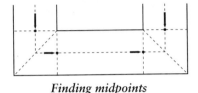

Finding midpoints

4. Measure the length of each border to find the midpoint. Make a midpoint mark on the border seam.

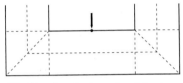

Finding border-length midpoint

SIZING A DESIGN TO FIT A BORDER

Border stencils and patterns seldom fit automatically within the borders of a quilt. There is a simple mathematical way to figure the adjustments you need to make a design fit a given area. Work through the following example using a quilt that measures 84" x 96". Figure each side separately.

1. Carefully measure the finished edge of one side of the quilt. For this example, use the 96" side.

2. Measure your quilting design from the outermost corner to the beginning of the first pattern repeat as shown. Make a note of this measurement. The example measures 9⁷⁄₈" which is equal to 9.875". Now measure the repeat itself—5.5".

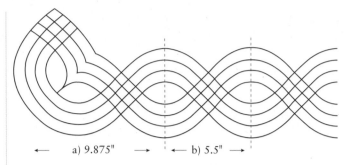

a) 9.875"   b) 5.5"

a) Measurment of outermost corner
B) Measurment of pattern repeat

3. Double the corner measurement to accommodate both corners on that side.
Example: 9.875" + 9.875" = 19.75" (19 3/4")

4. Subtract the measurement in Step 3 from the border length. Example: 96" - 19.75" = 76.25"

5. Into this measurement, divide the length of one pattern repeat (from Step 2). This tells you how many repeats you need to fill the border space.
Example: 76.25" ÷ 5.5" = 13.86

Since the answer is not a round number, you need to decide whether it is easier to shorten or lengthen the design. In this example, it is easier and more attractive to round down to 13 repeats, making each repeat longer.

6. Multiply the pattern-repeat measurement by the number of repeats needed.
Example: 13 repeats x 5.5" = 71.50"

7. Using the measurements from Steps 4 and 6, subtract the smaller from the larger. If Step 4 is larger, you'll need to lengthen the pattern repeat. If Step 6 is larger, you'll need to shorten the repeat.
Example: 76.25" − 71.50" = 4.75"

8. Divide the answer from Step 7 by the number of repeats needed for the border.
Example: 4.75 ÷ 13 = 0.365

This number tells you how much adjustment you need to make to each pattern repeat. In this example, .365 is just a hair less than $^3/_8$" (.375), so each pattern repeat will need to be made $^3/_8$" inch longer each time it is drawn.

9. Repeat Steps 1 through 8 for the top and bottom borders. In the example above, for the 84" top and bottom borders, it works out that the repeat must be $^1/_8$" longer each time.

10. Mark the center of the design repeat, or at the end of the channel nearest the center of the design repeat. With a different colored marker, draw a line $^1/_8$" to the side of this line. In the example, you are making the design longer, so draw the line to the left of the center line. Since the repeat in the longer border worked out to be slightly less than $^3/_8$" longer, draw yet another line in a different color $^3/_8$" from the center line. As you start to mark the design (a cable in the example shown below), mark to the center line, then slide the stencil to the right until the appropriate line for the border you are marking is aligned with the end of the lines you've drawn on the quilt, and continue. If the design needs to be shortened, mark the stencil the same way, but stop the marking line on the quilt at the center line instead of drawing to the end of a channel and sliding the stencil.

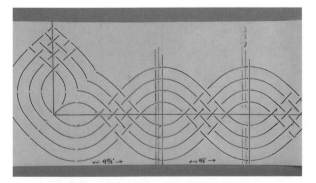

Cable stencil with marked lines. The black line is the center, the green line is the $^1/_8$" line, and the red line is the $^3/_8$" mark.

PAPER FOLDING TO FIT BORDERS

If you have a real aversion to math, you might prefer working with folded paper to resize your design. You will need a strip of paper the same length as the side of the quilt. Use Steps 1-3 of the formula on page 72 to determine this measurement. Once the strip of paper is cut to size, divide it into equal units. Now work with the cable-pattern repeat to determine what adjustments must be made in each unit. Draw the corrected repeats onto the paper for a complete border, or use one drawn section as a stencil. Transfer this to the quilt. Repeat for the top and bottom borders.

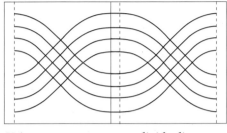

Using a paper pattern to divide distances

PREPARING BORDER STENCILS

Mark the registration lines directly onto the stencil with a permanent pen.

1. Draw a line to show the 45° angle of the corner.

2. Find the center of the design and draw a line the length of the stencil.

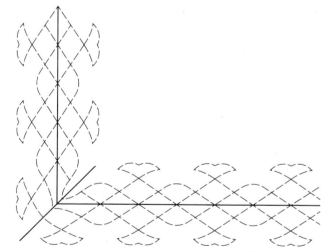

Registration lines on border stencil

These lines fall directly on top of the quilt registration lines. By having the register set, the stencil lines up with the borders and turns the corners accurately. When all the register lines are set, you are ready to mark the quilt top.

Marking Tools

There are many marking tools available—good and bad. It is your responsibility to make sure that the marker you choose is safe for the fabrics you are marking. As a consumer, you should be aware that even though a marking tool is identified as being for quilters, or is endorsed by a well-known quilter, there is no guarantee that the tool is safe to use under all conditions on all fabrics. What works perfectly in one situation may be disastrous for another. You may need to use different types of markers on a single quilt to get lines that show and are easily removed from all of the fabrics.

MARKING PENCILS

Traditionally, a graphite pencil was used to draw directly onto the quilt top. If you prefer this method of marking, the Berol Karismacolor Graphite Aquarelle, a water-soluble graphite pencil, seems to work well. I've found the medium lead works best. The point stays sharp and leaves a very light line when applied with a light touch. It is suitable for light solids, muslin, and white fabrics. Some quilters like hard-lead mechanical pencils, as they remain sharp. *Do not use a #2 soft graphite pencil. Cotton fabric tends to absorb the line and seldom releases it totally.*

There are a variety of markers available for light and print fabrics. These include:

Watercolor Markers: There are several brands of watercolor pencils available. They tend to be easily removed from fabric, but always test the various colors to be sure, particularly yellow. Watercolor pencils can leave a dark, bold line, so use a very light touch. Properly applied markings should wipe off easily with a damp cloth. Dixon Washout Cloth Markers are very good for marking prints and colors. They are available in red, green, white, and blue. The red and green are especially helpful for marking on darker prints.

Variety of colored markers

White Markers: There are several good white markers for use on dark fabrics. General Pencil Company's Charcoal White pencil is a very good choice, as is Schwan's CarbOthello white pastel pencil. Others to try include Roxanne Quilter's Choice, Nonce Marking Pencil, and General's Pastel Chalk pencils. *Always* pretest any product on your fabric to assure easy removal, and mark with a light but firm hand.

Tips

Dressmakers' white chalk pencils are made for marking the inside of garments, and include a high wax content. This makes markings difficult (if not impossible) to remove, so avoid these pencils for marking your quilt tops.

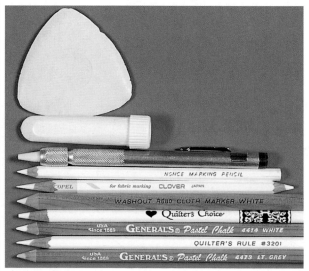
Variety of white markers

**Marking for Machine Quilting vs.
Marking for Hand Quilting**

Not all markers used by hand quilters work well for machine quilting. Hand quilters can work with fainter lines, because they don't have the visual obstructions posed by a machine. The machine head can limit your vision, and you are subject to working in shadows. You will also be quilting fairly quickly and need a marker that gives you a bold, easy-to-see and easy-to-remove line.

Remember: Although you want to see the lines, pressing too hard with any marker can spell trouble! Maintain an easy-to-mark finish by not prewashing your fabrics, or starch the fabrics to create a finish before you mark the quilt top. Then mark bold lines *with a light touch*. They'll be easier to remove later.

CHALKS AND POWDERS

Chalk Markers: White chalk contains no dye, so it is perfectly safe. It wipes off the surface of fabric easily; in fact, you might want to mark the quilt as you go. Exercise caution with red, blue, and yellow chalks as the dye in the chalk does not always wash out of the fabric or the quilting thread. Yellow can be especially troublesome because of the sulfur it contains. Always test first!

Tip

Spraying a marked area with hairspray can often keep the chalk in place for longer periods of time.

Pouncing Powder: Pouncing powder is an excellent method for marking flannel. It comes in small fabric-pouncing packets or pounce pads. Gently rub the pad over the stencil. The chalk is applied to the fabric through the stencil channels. As with chalk, I suggest that you mark the flannel quilt as you go, as the powder rubs off easily.

Pounce powder used to mark flannel

TESTING MARKING PENCILS

No matter what you may have heard about a product's reliability, test all marking devices you plan to use before marking the quilt top. Due to the variety of sizing and finishes on fabrics, as well as dye properties, each fabric can react differently to a specific marking tool. A pencil may be safe on every fabric in your quilt but one, but without testing, you won't know until it has ruined that fabric.

The test is simple. Perform it whether you prewash the fabrics or not.

1. Gather scraps of every fabric you will need to mark in the quilt and a variety of marking tools that show on each fabric. Starch the fabrics and mark lines on each scrap, making the line as dark as you need to see it readily.

2. Use a damp cloth or very soft toothbrush to rub gently along the fabric grain to remove the lines. If the lines come off easily, the marking tool is a good choice for that particular fabric. *Repeat this test with each fabric sample.*

Robbie Fanning suggests testing by running the samples through the wash. Mark a square of fabric with as many markers as show on the surface, number them, and make a list matching markers with the appropriate numbers. Cut each sample in half and wash half in the same water temperature and cleaning agent as you wash your quilts. Once the sample is dry, you will see which markers totally disappear, and have the unwashed sample as a reference.

▢ Avoid using fabric erasers. They lift an unsightly nap on the fabric. Also be careful of chemicals such as laundry pre-wash treatments, as they may cause color to run and ruin the quilt.

▢ Removing Graphite Lines

Apply the following mixture to the marking and rub gently with a soft toothbrush to remove graphite pencil as well as some colored-pencil lines. Follow by wiping with a cloth and then laundering.

1 part water

3 parts rubbing alcohol

1-2 drops Palmolive or Joy (not Dawn) dishwashing soap

WASH-OUT LIQUID MARKING PENS

Felt-tip liquid markers for quiltmakers have received a lot of bad publicity over the years, but they are one of the most useful markers available for machine quilting. Choices include Mark-B-Gone, Clover Water-Soluble Marker, and Clotilde's IBC Water-Erasable Blue Marking Pen. Try different brands until you find one with a tip that you like. Each has blue ink that is easy to see when following a design line, and disappears with water.

When they first appeared on the market, these were considered "miracle" markers, but soon reports of damaged fabrics began to surface. The problems, however, were caused by the user not removing the ink properly and thoroughly from the fibers of the fabric. These pens were developed for marking garments in dressmaking—items that are washed thoroughly. When used on quilts, but not removed properly, the lines can turn brown and become permanent. The chemical, if left in the fabric, weakens and breaks down the fibers.

Variety of wash-out markers

These pens are available with a regular or a fine-line tip. The regular tip gives a bold line that is easy to see. Do not press hard, but use a light touch instead. The ink will last much longer and the tip will stay sharper. Fine-tip pens make nice narrow lines for grid quilting—the narrower the marking, the morely likely you'll follow in a straight line—but they do tend to drag and skip on the fabric, so mark with a light touch. A starched quilt top is a real aid when you use these markers. The lines can be heat set, and therefore become permanent if ironed or exposed to high heat while still in the fabric.

I work with several pens at one time. I find that if I only use one pen, it dries out quickly. However, if I use one until the lines just begin to get pale, replace the cap tightly, store it cap down, and move on to another pen, the "resting" pen recharges and lasts much longer.

Tip

To help prevent dehydration, seal the pens in a resealable bag when not in use. The fine-line tips tend to dry out the fastest, so use them for a short time and rotate them often.

I have good luck using the blue markers on many dark fabrics. The line appears darker than the fabric and is quite easy to see with good light at the sewing machine. There are white felt-tip markers available as well. A light line appears a few seconds after marking on the fabric. The jury is still out as to how well they really work, but it is worth trying one.

Be especially careful of purple air-erasable pens. Strong light and humidity make the markings totally disappear; however, the chemical that remains in the fabric can cause permanent and unsightly damage if you do not remove it thoroughly.

REMOVING INK

After the quilting is finished, completely submerge the quilt in cold, clear water. Do not use soaps or detergents as the sodium content in the ingredients can set the lines. Soak the quilt until all the markings completely disappear, and then launder it in cool water and a neutral detergent such as Orvus Paste or Ivory to remove the chemical from the fibers. If you remove the ink properly, you should not have a problem with felt-tip pens. Once again, however, I recommend that you test all markers *before* you use them.

TESTING LIQUID MARKING PENS

Mark lines onto scraps of the fabrics you will mark in the quilt. I do this as I cut the fabrics for the quilt. I find that it takes me as long to piece and appliqué as to quilt, so the ink is in the fabric under similar conditions.

Once the top is finished, take the samples and soak them in cool, clear water until the markings disappear, and then wash them in soapy water. Follow with a rinse in cool water, then iron them dry with a hot iron. If the lines do not reappear in any way on a sample scrap, you are safe with that fabric. If the lines reappear when the scrap is ironed, the fibers have not released the chemical, and there is potential for damage.

Marking a Quilt Top

It's time to stress starch again: working with firm, crisp fabric makes the job of marking so much easier. Starch also puts a finish back onto prewashed fabrics, so when you draw lines onto the fabric, they are marked on the starch, not the fiber. This makes removal much easier and safer. The line washes away with the starch!

I try to do all the marking on the quilt top before I put the layers together and start to quilt. The only exception is when I am working with flannel and pounce powder, or fusible battings.

If you are using stencils to mark and are marking on a table, you might find the quilt top slips and shifts. An easy way to prevent this is by marking the top *while you are layering.* It is always easier to draw on two layers of fabric than on one. Center and secure the backing onto your layering table. (See page 79.) Lay out the quilt top directly onto the backing and mark the designs; the two layers of fabric will stick together. Once the top is marked, remove it from the backing and proceed with layering.

If you need a lightbox to trace the designs onto your quilt top, tape the paper pattern onto the surface of the lightbox before positioning the quilt top over it. You may also want to secure the quilt top to the lightbox to prevent minor shifting as you mark.

Many quilters have trouble quilting stencilled lines since the bridges leave blank spaces in the marked design. If it helps, draw in the missing sections to make the design one continuous line.

If you need to draw a very long, straight line and don't want to keep repositioning small grid stencils, consider using a carpenter's straight edge. These rulers come in various lengths and are typically much longer than a rotary ruler or yardstick. Another option is a plumb line. Fill the canister with pounce powder, position the string, stretch it tight, and snap a long, straight line.

> ### Tip
>
> Be sure to clean the edges of any straight edges or rulers before you use them to draw lines onto a quilt top. Ink from markers can pick up residue from previous marking tools (even permanent markers) from the edge of the ruler and transfer it to the fabric, causing a permanent line on the quilt.

Layering
and Pin-Basting

B e sure to read pages 24-25 for detailed information on layering tables, and pages 58-77 to make sure you have properly prepared the quilt top and backing for the layering process. In addition, review the checklist below before beginning.

▣ You have chosen the batting.

▣ You have squared, starched, and pressed the top well.

▣ You have carefully marked the quilting designs onto the quilt top.

▣ If necessary, you have pieced the backing fabric; it is starched and pressed.

If you have ever stretched and basted a quilt on the floor by the old, traditional methods, you will appreciate the method presented here: no more aching backs or sore knees.

Layering

▨ **NOTE:** *The backing and batting should be the same size: two to four inches larger than the quilt top.*

Starching the backing fabric and working on a table virtually eliminates all distortion and tucks on the backing. Starching and smoothing the backing before layering also controls any fullness that the feed dogs might translate into tucks and puckers. Successful layering is all in the preparation.

1. Create a work surface about three feet wide by five to six feet long. You might use a sheet of plywood, a counter top, the dining room table, or a similar surface. Avoid using ping-pong and pool tables, as they are too wide, and the backing fabric will not be stretched properly.

2. Measure the length and width of the table to find the center points on all four sides. Mark these centers with a toothpick. Place a piece of drafting tape over the toothpick so you can feel the bump through the layers of fabric as you work.

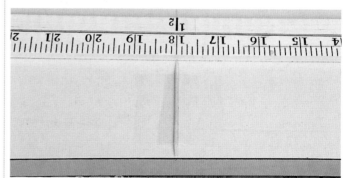

Using a toothpick to mark center of table

3. Fold the pieced, starched, and well-pressed backing in half lengthwise, wrong sides together. Also note the crosswise center, and place the backing on your work surface with the same amount of fabric hanging over each end. Place the folds on the toothpick guidelines.

Center backing on table to line up with toothpicks.

4. Unfold the backing to one thickness, wrong side facing up. Align the center of the backing with the center of the table. Allow the excess to hang off the edges.

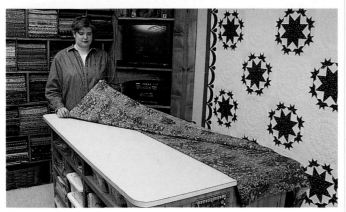

Open backing to lay flat on table.

5. Smooth and gently stretch the backing over the tabletop, using table basting clamps or any strong clip that fits the surface edge.

Tip

I use the term "stretch" with reservation. You often read instructions telling you to stretch the backing "drum tight." Please do not do this! You will very likely stretch and distort the grain of the fabric. Once you pin-baste and release the backing, the fabric will relax to its normal shape, causing reverse distortion. Tucks and puckers will be inevitable on the top and/or the bottom of the quilt. By starching the backing fabric heavily, you will eliminate much of the need to "stretch." Unstarched, limp fabric will creep and move on the table surface.

6. Begin by clamping one end of the backing with two or three clamps. Lightly smooth the fabric and clamp the opposite end, and then smooth and clamp the sides. Keep the backing as centered as possible, and use as many clamps as necessary to keep it smooth and slightly taut, but not overstretched. You should be able to run your hand over the fabric and see no movement or crawling, but there should be no stress on the grain of the fabric.

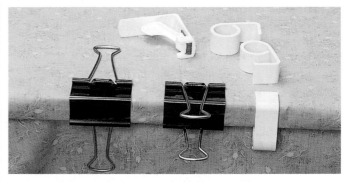

Variety of clamps for securing backing to table

Backing taut and secured to table

Tip

If the quilt or project is too small to clamp on one or more sides (for example, a block, small wall quilt, or baby quilt), use masking or drafting tape to tape the edges of the backing.

Taping a backing smaller than layering table

7. Fold the batting in half lengthwise, and smooth it free of fold lines and stretch marks. Check that the lengthwise grain of the batting is running in the same direction as the lengthwise grain of the backing.

Tip

Rx for Fold Lines

If polyester batting is distorted from packaging, place it in the clothes dryer on the very lowest heat setting. Toss in a damp hand towel, and tumble for ten to fifteen minutes. This should soften and remove the fold lines. Use steam from an iron to remove fold lines from natural fiber batts.

8. Place the batting on top of the backing, with the fold at the center placement guides (toothpicks). Unfold the batting so it hangs over the edges of the table. Smooth the batting out gently without stretching it.

Centering batting on backing

9. Now you are ready for the quilt top. Fold the quilt top in half lengthwise and crosswise, right sides together. Center the fold over the center placement guides, and open it so it hangs over the edges of the table. Be careful not to stretch the quilt top; just smooth it gently over the batting. The three layers— backing, batting, and quilt top—should now be centered and stacked. If you starched the top as you pieced it, it will be stiff enough to lay on the layers without the need for much manipulation.

Centering quilt top over batting

Quilt top smoothed over batting, ready to pin

Tip

Search for Stray Threads

Check the back of the quilt top for stray threads before layering it over the batting and backing. These threads can shadow through the fabric, and show from the top of the quilt. They are virtually impossible to remove once the layers are quilted. I have batting on my design wall, and find that as I place blocks on the wall, the surface becomes cluttered with stray threads. The batting acts as a magnet, so...I use a square of cotton batting to blot up the threads from the wrong side of the quilt top. It's so much easier than picking them off one by one!

Basting

Good basting technique is a very large contributor to the success of machine quilting. Whichever method you choose, make sure the quilt layers are secured tightly to prevent shifting. If you have not layered well, you will have endless trouble as you attempt to quilt on the machine.

BASTING TOOLS

Safety Pins: Safety pins stay in the quilt as it is rolled and rerolled throughout the quilting process. You'll need at least 350 safety pins to layer a double-size quilt; 500 or more for a king. Do not skimp on the number of pins!

I recommend #1, nickel-plated or rustproof safety pins to pin baste the layers together. (If you can find them in bulk, #0 pins are a little smaller and finer.) These pins are 1" long, with a fine tip that leaves a very small hole in the cloth. Large pins are easier to close, but leave damaging holes in the fabrics.

It is essential that the pins you choose are rustproof, as rust can cause permanent damage to the fabric. Some brass pins leave a black mark where they are inserted in the fabric. If you are unsure if your pins are rustproof, wrap a few in a wet piece of fabric and let the fabric dry. If the pins rust, do not use them in your quilt.

Tips

◙ Often you purchase a package that includes dull and/or rough pins. Keep a velvet emery strawberry in your pin box. The emery powder is abrasive, and perfect for sharpening and smoothing problem pins. Squeeze the strawberry tight and insert the pin in the hard area. Push the pin in and out a few times, and then twist it several times. If this doesn't work, toss the bad pins.

◙ Store your safety pins in a decorative tin. I keep a packet of silicone desiccant (from a shoebox) in the tin to keep away harmful moisture caused by humidity.

Safety-Pin Grips: This product, available at many quilt shops, makes safety pins very user-friendly. A safety-pin grip or cover is a molded piece of plastic that snaps over the top of the safety pin and acts as a handle. It gives your fingers more grip with less pressure, and makes the pin easier and more comfortable to manipulate.

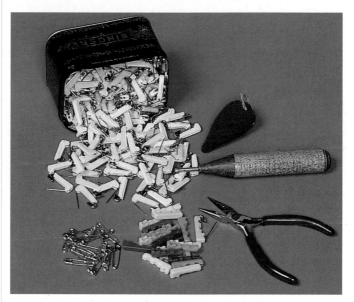

Basting tools: Kwik Klip, emery strawberry, and safety pins with covers

There are numerous other products to use when layering a quilt, such as the Quiltak Basting Tool and spray-basting glues. I personally do not find these products superior to pinning, and there are potential problems with each of them. I worry about the health issues involved with spray fixatives, as well as the possibility of a gummy needle, and layers that release during quilting. I have worked with several different brands and always go back to pins. The Quiltak may be very helpful if you have weak or damaged hands; however, always do a sample first. The needle is large and can put large holes in the fabric. I would avoid using this tool on fabrics such as sateen or batik. My best advice is that you try the options and make your own decision as to what works best for you.

PIN-BASTING

You might wonder why you can't just thread-baste as you would a hand quilting project. The answer is this: thread-basting does not hold up to machine quilting. You would need to baste very closely to keep the layers from shifting and bunching when you package and reroll the quilt. Basting threads can get caught in the foot as you quilt and are difficult to remove after machine stitching over them with many rows of machine quilting.

How far apart do you pin? My general guide is no further apart that the width of three knuckles, but you must also take into consideration the batting you have chosen.

On thin, cotton batting, place pins two to three inches apart. Cotton battings stick to the fabrics, and shifting of the layers is minimal. If you are using a thicker, more wiry polyester batting, or a wool batting, place the pins much closer (approximately one to three inches) together. These battings tend to shift a bit, and the more pins, the more control of the layers you will have. I can't stress enough how important preparation is, and pin-basting is one of the most important steps. Bottom line: pin, pin, pin!

Don't try to cut corners or eliminate any of the following steps when preparing the layers for the machine. This procedure keeps the layers from stretching, distorting, or tucking during the quilting process.

Start pinning in the center of the table, and work toward the edges and corners. Try to avoid pinning across seam lines that will be ditch quilted, or across any design lines. Place pins so that you can maneuver around them easily. Do not stretch and force any fabric to lay flat if it doesn't do so naturally. Ease in any fullness as you pin. (If your quilt tops continue to pose problems, go back and review pages 58-61.)

Placing safety pins through layers

Close the safety pins as you go. A grapefruit spoon or a tool called the Kwik Klip are invaluable for closing the pins. Both hold the fabric down while the pin goes through the layers. The pin's point comes back up into a groove that holds it secure, allowing you to simply push the top of the pin over the point and close it. No more sore and bloody fingers!

Using a Kwik Klip to close safety pins

Once the area on the tabletop has been pinned, remove the clamps from the layers on all sides of the table. Slide the quilt layers so that all but two inches of the pinned area is hanging off one side of the table. On the opposite side of the table, roll back the batting and quilt top. Gently smooth out the backing, using the pinned area as resistance. Reclamp the backing onto the table edge opposite the pinned area. Then stretch and reclamp the two remaining unpinned ends. You do not need to clamp the pinned side. The weight from the pins provides enough resistance to keep the backing stretched.

Repositioning quilt to one side

Reposition the batting and quilt top, smooth them, and pin the layers together from the pinned area to the opposite side. Continue until that side, then the other side, and then the ends of the quilt are completely pinned. (Once both sides are basted, you might want to rotate the quilt so the ends are placed on the length of the table, making it faster to stretch and pin-baste.) When the entire quilt is pin-basted, turn it over and run your hands over the backing. If any fullness backs up against a pin, you may need to unpin that area, reclamp it a bit tighter, and then repin to eliminate possible problems.

Packaging *and* Preparing to Quilt

A large top quilted on a home sewing machine requires special handling. This chapter covers methods of preparing and packaging your quilt to make the job easier. You will learn how to best prepare the quilt to go under the needle, and the basic steps of deciding which seams or areas to quilt first. Later chapters explain how to do the actual stitching techniques.

There are two guidelines I follow when preparing to quilt. If you keep these guidelines in mind, you'll manage the bulk and keep track of stitching order.

1. I never want to turn a quilt under the machine. Pushing the batting in too many directions can cause it to become distorted. In addition, it is very difficult, if not impossible, to successfully turn a large quilt and maneuver all the excess bulk through the rather small opening of the sewing machine.

2. I don't want more than half of the quilt under the machine at any time. I begin stitching on the center seamline or center row of blocks. Once that area is completed, I move to the next seam or row to the right, and so on. This allows me to continually unroll (and decrease) the bulk of the quilt under the arm of the machine, making the quilting easier. When I've finished quilting in one direction, I turn the quilt end-for-end and repeat the process for the other side.

Whenever possible, I suggest that you quilt your quilt in the ditch to stabilize the layers securely before proceeding to the more detailed quilting. Ditch quilting (page 104) is a machine-guided technique, and the most simple of all the quilting processes. Once the quilt is secured, you can remove many of the pins, making the quilt lighter in weight and easier to handle.

Packaging the Quilt

The first step in packaging the quilt is to lay it right side up on a table. Work from the center of the quilt to the right. Fold the left side of the quilt up to the center to within two inches of the seam or block you plan to quilt first. The left side of the quilt will be supported by the table.

Roll the right side of the quilt as tightly as you can, also to within two inches of the center. This is the side that goes through the machine arm and must be rolled tightly so that it fits. Now you will see what a difference batting thickness makes in your ability to work a large quilt under the machine. If the batting is thick and fluffy, the roll is so large that it barely fits, and limits your space to maneuver. A thin batting is much easier to work with in a large quilt.

If the right side keeps coming unrolled, it can create problems as you try to feed the quilt through the machine. There are a variety of aids available to help you with this.

Bicycle pant-leg clips, also known as Quilter's Clips, work well to hold the roll in place. These clips are made of spring steel and go around the large roll to secure it. Be sure that you get oval clips, not round ones: they stay in place much better. Covering them with twill tape keeps them from sliding and scratching your machine.

In addition to metal clips, you will also find various clips made from sliced PVC pipe, or different plastic clips such as Jaws. Look for clips in a size that corresponds with the size of your quilt.

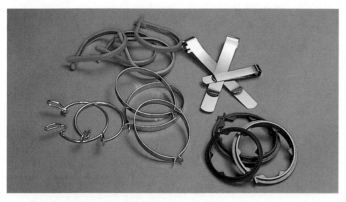

Variety of clips for holding large quilts

You'll find these clips most helpful when you are ditch quilting. (The roll does not collapse as the length of the quilt extends behind the machine.) As you unroll the quilt to the right for each successive quilting line, you can unroll from inside the clips; you do not need to remove them each time. This speeds up the process immensely.

Place the clips down the length of the quilt, using a sufficient number to control the quilt. You will generally need four to twelve clips for a large quilt.

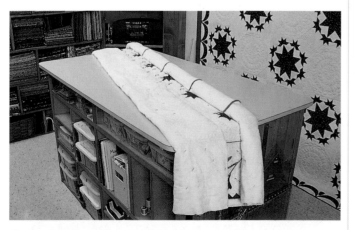

Packaging the quilt to go through the machine

Once the sides of the quilt are under control, figure how you can best manage the length. If the quilt is fairly small, you can fold the length into accordion pleats, making a compact package to put in your lap. The quilt will unfold automatically as you work.

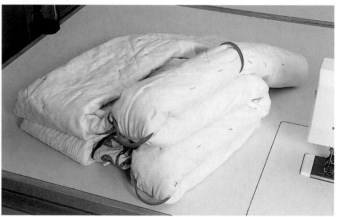

Accordion pleats

Sit down at the machine with the package in your lap. Place the quilt under the machine at the beginning of the line you wish to quilt, and insert the needle. Adjust the quilt in your lap. Unroll or unfold a couple of rolls or pleats and "punch" the fabric to rest on your chest so the quilt is feeding down into the machine, not dragging up from your lap. Now you are ready to stitch.

Holding quilt in lap, punched up to feed into machine

If the quilt is too large to hold in your lap, try throwing it over your left shoulder. This position lets the quilt feed down into the machine at a good angle, and you can wrap your arm around it as you quilt.

Over-the-shoulder position for supporting quilt

Tip

Avoid wearing cotton or other natural-fiber shirts or tops if you work with the quilt slung over your shoulder, as the quilt will cling to you, making progress difficult. Instead, wear a garment that allows the quilt to slide smoothly from your shoulder.

One of my students shared this method of supporting the quilt while keeping the weight off her body. You might want to try it. Insert an eighteen inch café-curtain rod through a small PVC pipe that allows the rod to roll. Tie a rope to both ends, and suspend it from a hook in the ceiling above your shoulder. This allows the quilt to

be in the proper position, but off your shoulder. You can even get up and walk away, come back, and start right where you left off with the quilt in the correct position.

Another method that might work for you is to keep a table or lowered ironing board at your left side, the same height as your sewing cabinet. You can lay the quilt on the table and bring it into the machine under your left arm. This eliminates having the bulk of the quilt on you as you work.

Table on left to support quilt under arm

Some quilters tell me that they let the quilt hang off onto the floor on their left side, pull a large portion of it into their lap, and feed the quilt into the machine from this position.

Quilt under arm and falling to floor, supported on chest

Obviously, there is no one right way to handle the bulk of a large quilt. Try a variety of options to see which one works best for you. Often a combination of ideas is the key to success. Experiment with a few practice runs to get comfortable with the weight and bulk before you actually begin stitching.

PACKAGING FOR DIAGONAL QUILTING

If you plan to quilt diagonal lines in a quilt, use the same packaging technique as described on page 85, but roll the right side in from a corner, and fold the left side from the opposite corner. Instead of folding the length of the quilt into a square package, throw it over your left shoulder and feed it into the machine. When folded diagonally, the quilt package tends to open, so using your shoulder and arm to keep the sides rolled and the quilt feeding consistently into the machine is really helpful.

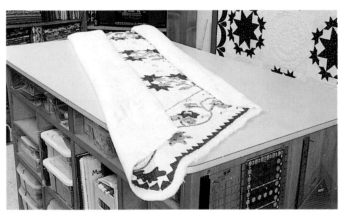

Packaging a diagonally set quilt

Experiment with the different packaging processes, and get started. Don't let the size of the quilt intimidate you. Once you get it under the machine, you'll soon find what you need to do to handle the bulk. Your main goal is to keep any drag or weight of the quilt away from the area you are stitching. Don't worry if your work area is not as neat and tidy as the photos show. Remember: they are photos taken for a book!

Organizing a large quilt for ditch quilting

PACKAGING FOR FREE-MOTION QUILTING

When you ditch quilt, the packaging is pretty straight forward. However, when you start to quilt large areas with free-motion quilting, things get messy. You need to unroll the right side to accommodate movement to the right to follow a pattern, and do the same thing with the left roll or fold. Create a "well" around the needle area, and the rest of the quilt will bunch up so it glides easily with your hand motions.

You move your hands and the fabrics quite a bit with free-motion quilting, so freedom of movement is crucial. You will occasionally need to reposition the bunched-up quilt so your hands can continue to move the "well" area easily. This is why you need such a large working surface!

Quilt supported by table surface for free-motion quilting

Where Do You Start Quilting?

Whenever possible, stabilize the quilt with ditch quilting before any adding other quilting. This gives you more control of the layers as you get into more detailed quilting techniques. I recommend using invisible nylon thread for this step, so the stitching is totally invisible when done well.

ANCHORING THE LAYERS TOGETHER

Anchoring is the first step in ditch or grid quilting a project. This keeps the layers straight and free of distortion as you proceed with additional quilting. Quilt the anchor seams first. These include the very center seamlines in the quilt, both lengthwise and crosswise. By securing these two lines first, you'll be able to tell if the foot or feeding system is pushing any fabric or batting forward. If a tuck appears when you cross an anchor line, you'll know the foot is not feeding properly, you have not layered well, or you are not feeding the fabric correctly.

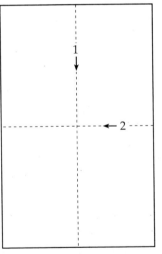

Anchoring lines

Tip

If there is no seam in the very center of the quilt, move to the first seam to the right of the center.

When deciding on which seam to anchor first, consider where the grainlines of the batting and backing fall. Quilt the seam that runs with that lengthwise grain first to eliminate possible stretching and distortion in the finished quilt. For example, if the lengthwise grainline of the batting and backing runs the length of the quilt, quilt the lengthwise center seam (or first seam to the right) first. If the lengthwise grainline runs across the width of the quilt, quilt the center crosswise seam (or first seam to the right) first.

> **NOTE:** *The seams identified above are the structural seams that join the key elements of the quilt top; that is, the seams that join the blocks, or the seams that join blocks to sashing. You are not quilting seams within the blocks at this time.*

1. Quilt the lengthwise seam (or crosswise seam depending on the backing and batting grainline), starting just inside the border seam, or at the edge of the quilt if there is no border. Stitch from the one end to the other end of the quilt (1 on illustration at left).

2. Next, refold and reroll the quilt so the center crosswise seam is exposed (or lengthwise seam depending on the backing and batting grainline). This is the second anchor seam (2 at left). Stitch from one side to the opposite side of the quilt. This completes the anchoring seams.

Do not start quilting in the center of the quilt and stitch out in both directions. This can cause heavy distortion in the center of the quilt, creating an umbrella effect where all the stitching starts and stops.

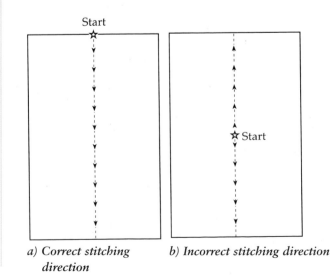

a) Correct stitching direction *b) Incorrect stitching direction*

When I do really close ditch or grid quilting, I find I have better control of the layers and am more able to prevent shifting if I add a crosswise anchor line at the top center and bottom center of the quilt before I return to do the remaining lengthwise seams. This gives me three lines to cross every time I quilt a lengthwise seam. I can readily see if fabric is shifting, and make the necessary adjustments of more pinning, relayering, or working with my walking foot differently.

DIAGONALLY SET QUILTS

Diagonally set quilts are a bit more difficult to quilt than straight sets, as you are stitching bias through the backing and batting, as well as the quilt top. If you are inexperienced with machine quilting, I recommend that you not start the learning process on a diagonally set quilt. Once you have the technique down and know how to control the walking foot, you shouldn't have any problems with diagonal quilting.

If the quilt top is a square and the blocks are set on the diagonal, anchor the layers by quilting from one corner to the opposite diagonal corner. If the block seams run right into the corner, begin stitching in the very corner of the quilt, as shown in illustration (a). More often, there is a block in the corner, so the seam won't run right to the corner, but off to the side. In this case, stitch the seam to the right of the corner, as shown in the illustration (b). Repeat the process for the opposite corners. This makes an X across the quilt.

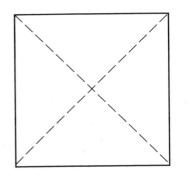

a) Anchoring a square-grid pattern

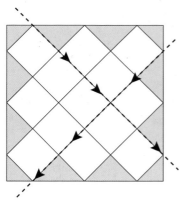

b) Anchoring a square diagonally set quilt

If the quilt is longer than it is wide, make two Xs so all four corners are stitched, using the example most appropriate to the layout of the blocks.

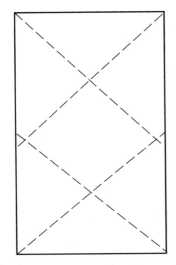

Anchoring a rectangular diagonal set

Proceed the same as for lengthwise and crosswise seams. Stitch from the center out to a corner, turn the quilt end-for-end and repeat for the opposite side. Rotate the quilt and continue with the remaining sides.

DITCH QUILTING

Once you have anchored the quilt, you are ready to continue with the remaining seams. Reroll the quilt lengthwise once again. Continue to stitch the seams to the right of center until you reach the border.

1. Begin each stitching line at the top border or edge and continue down through the anchor line to the bottom border or edge. Lock off the stitches at the beginning and end of every seam. Unroll the quilt to the next line, fold up the left side a bit more, and quilt the next line to the right from top to the bottom. Continue until the side is completed.

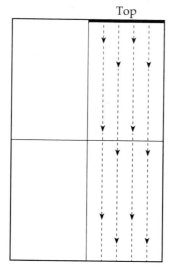

Stitching each line to the right of the center

Tip

If you must jump over an area, such as sashing, where there is no seam for a short distance, lock off the stitches at the end of the seam, lift the presser foot, drag the thread to the next seam on the other side of the obstruction, lock the stitches, and proceed.

2. Repackage the quilt so the roll on the right side includes the unquilted, lengthwise seams, and the fold on the left includes the previously quilted area. The quilt is now turned quilt end-for-end, so the true bottom of the quilt is in the top position. Repeat Step 1, working to the right, until all the lengthwise lines are stitched.

NOTE: *I have heard it suggested that you go back and forth from one side to the other when at this stage of quilting. When you really think this through, you'd be working twice as hard. No matter what order you stitch in, you still can't have more than half the quilt under the machine. You are simply repackaging the quilt twice as often to rotate back and forth, in effect working twice as hard to achieve the same thing.*

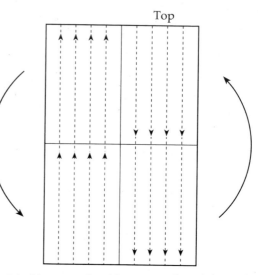

Stitching opposite side; turn quilt end-for-end

3. Quilt the crosswise seams next. Repackage the quilt so the crosswise seams are ready to be quilted. The quilting becomes easier because the layers are now well-secured by the lengthwise seams, and it's not possible for the crosswise grain to move or stretch. Continue to use the walking foot to eliminate all tucks at the seam crossings. Quilt from the center out to the right, top to bottom, until all seams are quilted. Rotate the quilt so the other side is now on your right (top) and repeat.

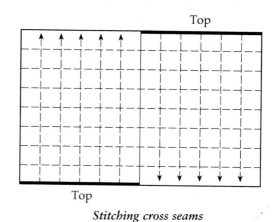

Stitching cross seams

Tip

Quilting Border Seams

I quilt the seams that attach the border at the same time I quilt the lengthwise and crosswise seams in Steps 1-3 (above). This eliminates having to turn corners with the foot later, which can push the batting slightly, and cause the corners to stretch or cup up.

4. Ditch quilt any diagonal seams last. The natural stretch of bias will no longer be a problem because you've created stability with the straight-grain quilted seams.

TEMPORARY DITCH QUILTING

Anchoring is essential to trouble-free machine quilting. I learned this lesson the hard way after really messing up a quilt with close diagonal-grid quilting. I didn't want the visible depression created in the seams by ditch quilting, so I just pinned securely and started stitching the diagonal grid from the center out. Problems arose when I needed to start and stop at trapunto feathers in the sashings. Because there was not enough stabilization, the fabric started to push slightly without my knowing it. When I came to the barrier of the feathers, the surface started getting tiny tucks. When I tried to ease in the fabric, it developed unsightly ripples.

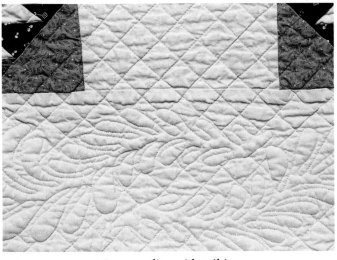

Poor-quality grid quilting

I was too far into the quilt to rip it all out, so I have to live with it! But I did come up with a solution afterward: ditch quilting the entire quilt with YLI Wash-A-Way thread top and bobbin. It totally secures the layers, eliminating any chance of the diagonal quilting causing distortion. When the quilt is washed, the ditch-quilting stitches dissolve away and the quilt looks just the way it should. Magic! Give it a try to stabilize the quilt at those times you think ditch quilting might detract from the final look.

The Next Steps

If ditch quilting is all you plan for your quilt, you are finished. However, if it is primarily intended to secure the layers before adding free-motion surface quilting designs, continue on.

ADDING FREE-MOTION DESIGNS

There are a couple of different ways to approach free-motion quilting. If you have ditch quilted the entire quilt, you can begin on the outside row of blocks and move into the center of the quilt. You can remove many of the pins and have much more freedom to glide around the marked designs and background areas. Since the structural quilting holds the layers so securely, you won't cause distortion by working "backward." As a benefit, the quilting compresses the batting, making the roll smaller and smaller, giving you more room under the arm of the machine to function, and making the quilt much easier to manage.

I do not quilt the borders first. I prefer to leave them for last and work continuously around the perimeter of the quilt without having to stop and start at corners. Many border designs have no breaks in them, so doing them last is an advantage.

> **Tip**
>
> **Free-Motion Freedom**
>
> Once you are comfortable with free-motion quilting, you might choose to ditch quilt using the darning foot. This eliminates the need for careful feeding, and you can start and stop anywhere the design dictates. I still prefer to use the walking foot to do the hard work of long straight lines through the whole quilt. But for short, curvy, or angled seams within blocks, I use the darning foot for free-motion quilting. I can go any direction I need to without turning the quilt. Such freedom!

If you don't stabilize the layers with ditch quilting, start at the center row of blocks and quilt down that row. The layers are stabilized by the pins and your hands only, so you'll need to work very carefully. Follow the same order of stitching as ditch quilting. Once the center row is finished, proceed to the next row of blocks to the right. When one side of the quilt is finished, flip it around, package up to the centermost row that needs to be quilted, and continue until that side is done. Now you are ready for borders.

I find it very helpful to stitch around the perimeter of the border with the darning foot, basting the layers. Since the darning foot does not use a feeding system, the layers are not distorted in any way. If you cut the borders wider than needed as suggested on page 61, baste just inside the drawn trimming line. If you do not cut away the basting stitches, the edge will be held securely when you attach the binding.

STITCHING ORDER

There is a definite order in which to work through a quilt. Jumping from area to area and technique to technique only creates uneven stitches, distortion of the quilt, and fatigue for the quilter.

When you are planning your quilting strategy, consider all the elements you plan for the quilting. If you do them in order, and complete one process at a time, you take advantage of the stabilization provided by ditch quilting and build up a good rhythm by the repetition of each technique.

Here is the game plan for a pieced quilt:
1. Ditch quilt all the structural seams within the quilt top. You can use water-soluble thread if you don't want this stitching to be permanent. This is really helpful if all the quilting will be done in diagonal grids.

2. Complete any other quilting that requires the walking foot.

3. Free-motion quilt all the designs within blocks and sashing strips.

4. Quilt any continuous curves in pieced blocks.

5. Stitch any grid quilting or echo quilting in the background of blocks.

6. Stipple quilt any background areas.

7. Quilt the borders.

Here is the order for quilting appliqué quilts:
1. Ditch quilt all structural seams within the quilt top.

2. Use the darning foot to ditch quilt around each element of every appliqué.

3. Grid, stipple, or echo quilt any background area around the appliqués.

4. Quilt the borders.

Here is the order for quilting borders:
1. If you are quilting the border with all straight lines, especially on the diagonal, start in the center of one border and work in one direction to the corner on the right. Return to the center and quilt the lines to the left. (These may be quilted at a different angle.) If the design is a grid, quilt the intersecting grid lines after the entire length has been quilted in one direction. This keeps the border from stretching too much in one direction.

2. If the border includes a cable or other motif, quilt the design first, and then add background stitching such as grid work or echo quilting.

3. Stipple the background area if desired.

You will need to analyze each quilt top that you make to figure out your approach. Much of this planning is covered on pages 58-66. You might want to review these chapters as you determine the most successful strategy.

Gallery:
ADVANCED-LEVEL QUILTS

Kretsinger's Last Rose

73" x 74", hand appliquéd and machine quilted by Julie Yaeger Lambert, Erlanger, KY.

From the quilt designed by Rose Kretsinger (pattern in *Quilters' Newsletter Magazine,* issue 292). Mountain Mist Blue Ribbon cotton batting; 50/3 Mettler "Silk Finish" cotton thread on top and in the bobbin.

Spoon River Christmas

*85" x 85", pieced and quilted
by Jean Lohmar, Galesburg, IL.*

Jean used free-motion and stippling techniques.
Fairfield Cotton Classic batting; 60/2 Mettler
cotton embroidery thread in both top and in
the bobbin.

Looking Up
82" x 82", pieced and quilted by Cynthia Schmitz, Arlington Heights, IL.
Based on her original quilting design, ditch, free-motion, and stippling techniques were used. Fairfield Cotton Classic batting; Quilters Dream Poly batting for trapunto; invisible nylon thread on top; Madeira Tanne 50/2 cotton embroidery thread in bobbin.

Empty Nest II

85" x 93", pieced and quilted by Barbara A. Perrin, Pullman, MI. Pattern from Legacies of Love *by Susan H. Garman.*

Channel and straight-line quilting, free-motion, stippling, and trapunto techniques were used. Features two hundred fifty-five $3^5/_8$" stars! Hobbs Heirloom Premium cotton-blend batting; Fairfield Poly-Fil Extra-Loft batting for trapunto; YLI Wonder Invisible thread (both smoke-colored and clear) on top; 50/3 Mettler "Silk Finish" cotton thread in the bobbin for straight lines; 60/2 Mettler embroidery thread in the bobbin for stippling and trapunto.

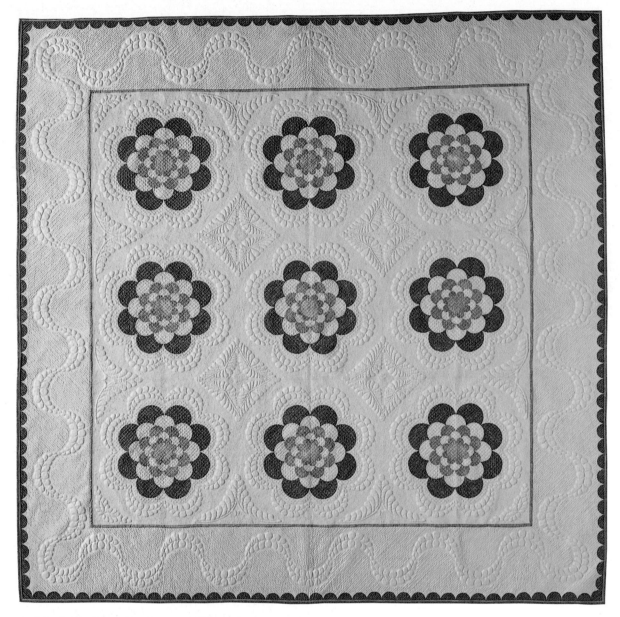

Pride of the Prairie
84" x 84", appliquéd and quilted by Jean Lohmar, Galesburg, IL.

Jean used invisible machine appliqué, grid, tiny echo, free-motion, trapunto, stippling, and channel-quilting techniques. Cotton sateen gives the background a soft luster. Fairfield Cotton Classic batting; Quilters Dream Poly Select batting for trapunto; Mettler 60/2 embroidery thread and clear nylon thread on top; 60/2 Mettler embroidery thread and Madeira Cotona 80 wt. thread in the bobbin.

Primrose Star

85" x 102", Pieced by Nancy Barrett, Edmond, OK. and quilted by Harriet Hargrave.

This quilt features ditch, channel, free-motion, continuous-curve, and echo-quilting techniques. Adapted from a 1925 quilt by Bonnie Irwin Carden. Hobbs Heirloom Premium cotton-blend batting; 50/2 DMC embroidery thread in top and in the bobbin.

Rich's Millennium Star

63" x 84", pieced and quilted by Barbara A. Perrin of Pullman, MI. Pattern from Legacies of Love *by Susan H. Garman.*

This quilt has heavy straight-line quilting over the stars and free-motion, stippling, and trapunto techniques in the border. Hobbs Polydown batting; Fairfield Poly-Fil Extra-Loft batting for trapunto; YLI Wonder Invisible thread on top and 50/3 Mettler "Silk Finish" cotton thread in the bobbin for pieced areas; 50/3 Mettler "Silk Finish" cotton thread and 60/2 Mettler embroidery thread on top and in the bobbin for free-motion designs and stippling.

Bill's Blue Star
79" x 103", pieced and quilted by
Julie Yeager Lambert, Erlanger, KY.
Julie used ditch, grid, and free-motion techniques.
Quilters Dream Cotton batting; 50/3 Mettler "Silk
Finish" cotton thread on top and in the bobbin.

Feathered-Edge Star,
*64" x 64", Blocks pieced by Charla Gee,
Littleton, CO. and quilted by Harriet
Hargrave.*

Inspired by a tattered antique, this quilt is quilted
with ditch, grid, free-motion and padded-quilting
techniques. Mountain Mist Blue Ribbon cotton batting; Sew-Art International Invisible Nylon clear
thread and Superior Threads Bottom Line on top;
60/2 Mettler embroidery thread in the bobbin.

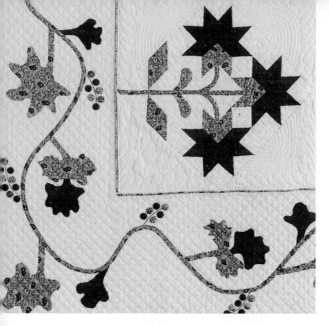

Double Peony

66" x 80", Blocks pieced by Charla Gee, Littleton, CO. and appliquéd and quilted by Harriet Hargrave.

This quilt features channel quilting in the pieced blocks, free-motion techniques in the alternate blocks, and $1/2$" grid quilting in border. Reproduction of an 1840s quilt in Harriet's collection. Mountain Mist Natural 100% Cotton batting; Sew-Art International Invisible Nylon clear thread on top; 60/2 Mettler embroidery thread in the bobbin.

PART THREE

QUILTING TECHNIQUES

Straight-Line Quilting: *Ditch Quilting*

CHAPTER 9

NOTE: *Preparation is everything if you really want to become a good machine quilter. Please take the time to study the first eight chapters. I can't stress enough the importance of that basic information in achieving success with the skills taught in the next four chapters.*

The easiest and most basic form of machine quilting is quilting in the ditch. This is more of a structural technique than a decorative technique. Ditch quilting is often used to anchor the seams between the blocks before surface quilting within the blocks. This makes the quilt much more stable and easier to control under the machine's foot.

Ditch quilting can also stand alone as the only quilting applied to the layers. Many quilt tops do not require fancy surface quilting. If the pieced design is very strong, or if the pattern on the fabric is busy and dominant, the quilting generally won't show. Stitching in-the-ditch is a functional and easy way to secure the three layers together.

You can make ditch quilting temporary by using water-soluble thread. It is an excellent way to secure the layers together and eliminate any chance of distortion when you are doing extensive diagonal grid work. Once the quilting is finished, the lines of ditch quilting dissolve away, leaving no depression in the seam. Refer to page 91 for more on this subject.

Preparing to Ditch Quilt

A walking foot makes stitching the long, straight lines of ditch quilting very easy. This foot uses a feeding system, so you must take care to keep the layers from shifting by layering properly.

As you plan the order of quilting, make certain you won't need to turn the quilt under the machine, and so that only half of the bulk is under the machine at any time.

Review pages 58-61 thoroughly for detailed information about pressing seams. Good pressing holds the seam in position so the walking foot can feed evenly, and so the needle can come close enough to the ditch for the stitching to remain invisible. Poorly pressed seams hinder even your best efforts to create invisible stitching.

To locate the ditch, rub your thumb across the seam. On one side, you will feel a ridge created by the bulk of the seam allowance. The side opposite this ridge is a single thickness of fabric. When ditch quilting, you'll need to keep the needle on this low side, actually rubbing the edge of the ridge as you stitch. When the seam is quilted and the fabric relaxes, the stitching is completely hidden in the fold.

Needle in ditch on the low side of seam, rubbing fold of seam allowance

I always use nylon thread for ditch quilting. As noted on page 45, the size of the needle can affect how much the stitching shows. If the needle is too wide, it will stitch just far enough away for the stitches to show when the needle rubs the edge of the seam. With nylon thread, you can use a smaller needle, such as a 60/8 or 65/9, to keep the stitches totally invisible. Cotton thread requires a larger needle so there is no way to hide the stitches.

a) Large needle with nylon thread

b) Large needle with cotton thread

c) Small needle with nylon thread

Imperfect piecing can cause problems with ditch quilting. When you are ditch quilting, you need to keep the quilting in-the-ditch—and hidden—at all times. If the intersections of the pieces, blocks, or sashing strips do not butt perfectly, there is a tendency to shift from one ditch to another at the intersection. As a result, the stitches are visible on the surface of the quilt.

The photo below shows a seam that is perfectly butted. The top seam is pressed to the left and the bottom seam is pressed to the right. As you start stitching on the top section, the ditch will be on the right side of the seam. At the intersection, the ditch shifts to the left side of the seam. Because the seam is perfectly butted, you will simply "fall" into the left side of the seam as you stitch. Since the seam is a continuous straight line, the stitching stays totally hidden.

Perfectly butted seam; straight line to quilt

When the intersection is not perfectly butted, as in the next photo, you must deal with a gap or overlapped area at the intersection. While you'll obviously want to avoid this problem with perfect piecing, there is a way to cope once you've reached the quilting stage. Start at the top and stitch down the right side of the seam. When you come to the intersection, stop the needle where the horizontal and top vertical seams intersect. Take two or three stitches in the same hole, either by lowering the feed dogs or setting the stitch length on zero. Lift the needle and the presser bar. Move the quilt to the left (or right), just enough to place the needle in the intersection of the horizontal and bottom vertical seam. Take two or three stitches in the same hole, and then raise the feed dogs or go back to your original stitch length. I call this maneuver a "side step."

Seam not butted correctly; must side-step when quilting seam

Resume stitching on the left side of the seam. You will have a tiny stitch in the horizontal seam at this point, which is preferable to seeing stitches on the surface, "aiming" from one seam to another. While this technique does slow the process of ditch quilting, the result is well worth the effort. Practice on a sample block until you get the hang of it.

NOTE: *Be sure to take more than one stitch in the horizontal seam. If you use the needle-down function on your sewing machine, the stitch may skip as you move to the side, leaving an angled thread visible across the intersection.*

LOOKING AT THE NEEDLE

Before you start the stitching process, get comfortable with where you are sitting and what you must train your eye to focus on. (This is definitely a process of eye/hand coordination.) Sit directly in front of and centered with the needle, high enough so you can look directly down onto the needle as it enters the fabric.

> ### Tip
>
> Many sewing-machine dealers and teachers advise you to use an edge-stitching foot for ditch quilting. I don't recommend this. Instead, use a walking foot and keep your eye on the needle! Don't forget how important it is to cut a wider opening between the toes of your walking foot to make an open-toe foot (page 30).

Mount the walking foot onto your machine and lower the presser bar so the feeders are sitting on the feed dogs. Lower the needle into the machine. There is generally a line or small opening in front of the foot, between the toes, to denote the center of the foot. See if the needle lines up perfectly with this mark; it more than likely does not.

Now think of how you sew. You generally align the foot with the fabric. If you place the foot on the fabric and align the marking of the foot exactly with the seam, but the needle is not also in line with the foot, the stitching won't be in the ditch! Also, if you look at the line and the seam, and adjust the quilt so that both remain in alignment, you are again taking the needle out of position.

Start training your eyes to look at the needle. Make sure the needle is rubbing the seam, every stitch of the way. If you are ditch quilting properly, you are focused on the needle, disregarding where the foot is in relation to the seam. This will seem awkward at first because you are used to the "sewing mode." You have spent years looking at the foot to guide fabric through your machine. But you are now going to learn to **_hand quilt with an electric needle._**

If you are working on a Pfaff with the built-in dual feed, use the open-toe appliqué foot instead of the general-purpose foot. It will give you unobstructed vision.

QUILTING A TRIAL BLOCK

Before starting any project, make it a habit to test your machine on a sample of the fabric and batting you've used in the quilt. Once this sandwich is made, quilt a few rows of stitches, checking that the tension and stitch length are to your liking.

Start by stitching several seams in your sample block using various stitch lengths. A desirable length is similar to the length you prefer in hand quilting—generally about eight to fifteen stitches per inch. A stitch that is too short will perforate and weaken the fibers, and can cause tearing when stress is applied to the quilt. A stitch that is too long will break when stress is applied, and is more difficult to control as you sew.

You'll also want a stitch that looks as good on the back of the sample as it does on the front; check the back of the sample to be sure that the stitches are consistent in length. If the stitches are erratic, your walking foot may not be mounted properly, you may be pushing the fabric too much rather than allowing the foot to do all the feeding, or your walking foot may be hanging up on the bulk of seam allowances.

Tip

Any time you change the stitch length on your machine you can affect the tension, so be sure to double check before you proceed, and adjust your tension accordingly. You want a perfectly balanced tension, with no loops of bobbin thread showing on the top, and no loops of top thread showing on the back.

Ditch-Quilting Technique

Learn this techique by practicing on a sample block or small quilt. Once you've worked out all the details, you'll do a wonderful job of ditch quilting your quilt top.

NOTE: *Be sure to review pages 88-92 regarding grainline, stitching order, and so on.* **This information is critical to the success of keeping your quilt flat, square, and distortion free.**

Begin with the center seam that runs with the lengthwise grain of the batting and backing. Position the packaged quilt so this center seam, or the first seam to the right of the center, is exposed. Accordion pleat the quilt from the bottom up if it is small enough, or throw the excess over your left shoulder. Place the top edge under the machine.

BEGINNING TO STITCH

If you are beginning on the outside edge of the quilt, hold both the top and bobbin threads tightly as you begin to stitch.

Holding both top and bottom threads at raw edge

If there is a border or sashing strip around the block, begin the stitching inside the border at the border seamline.

Holding both threads on surface inside border seam

Bring the bobbin thread to the surface before beginning to stitch. With the presser bar down, take one complete stitch, either manually with the hand wheel or by using the automatic needle-up position. Make sure that the take-up lever is in its highest position when you stop. This assures that the top thread is no longer wrapped around the bobbin shuttle and can be pulled to the top easily. Raise the foot, move the fabric over slightly, and pull on the top thread from both sides of the needle hole. The bobbin thread should appear through the hole; pull it through. Continue to hold both the top and bobbin threads as you insert the needle into the ditch, and lower the walking foot.

Lock off the thread tails before starting to quilt. Note that stitching in place and backstitching are not the best methods for locking the thread into the fabric. Nylon thread is slick, and will slip out of these stitches. Cotton threads make an unsightly lump. Instead, follow these instructions to bury a $1/4$" line of very tiny stitches in the ditch, critical when using nylon thread.

1. Set the stitch length on $1/2$ or .5 on a digital machine (about 50 stitches per inch). Stitch for $1/4$" at this setting. These stitches are so small that they cannot pull out, and virtually disappear into the weave of the fabric.

2. Once you've locked off the stitching, clip the thread tails even with the surface of the fabric. This keeps you from having to weave the threads back into the batting or tying them off.

> ### Tip
>
> **Program for Locking Stitches**
> If you are working on a computerized machine, you may be able to program a stitch to use as your lock-off setting throughout the quilting process. Choose the zigzag stitch, and set the stitch length at $1/2$ or .5 and the stitch width at 0. Push the button for straight stitch. Set the stitch length control for your chosen length. Now push the zigzag button again. Did it keep the new settings? Many machines have short-term memory capabilities that allow you to make these adjustments without using any memory function. Try it. It makes locking off so much easier. I use my #1 and #2 stitch buttons. When I'm starting to quilt, I press #2 (the zigzag button with the new settings) and stitch for $1/4$". Then I press #1, and I am ready to quilt the seam. At $1/4$" from the end of the seam, I press #2 again and am set automatically for the tiny stitches. What a time saver!

3. Move the length regulator to the setting you found suitable on your sample, generally a stitch-length setting of $2^1/2$-3, or 8 to12 stitches per inch.

As you begin stitching, do not "help" the machine more than necessary by pushing, shoving, and pulling the fabric through the foot. This just causes distortion and tucks. Train your hands to work with the fabric and the foot. Do not push and pull.

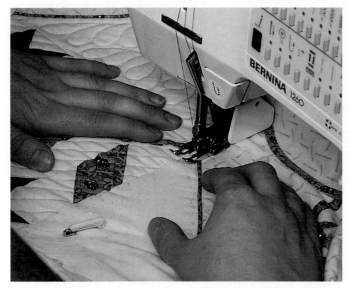

Incorrect hand placement; don't pull at seam or push quilt through machine

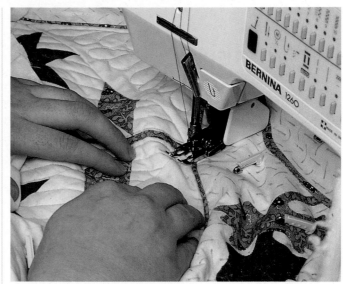

Correct hand placement, using fingers to feed top layer to walking foot

You may notice that the top layer wants to push ahead a bit, causing a small tuck to appear when you come to a seam. You can eliminate this by feeding the excess fabric back toward the foot while you stitch the length of the seam. Work with only the one to two inches of fabric directly in front of the needle at any time.

Position your thumbs about three inches in front of the foot and apply a bit of pressure. Let your fingertips gently push any fullness *of the top layer only* back toward the foot. Be careful that you do not also push the batting and backing. As you stitch, allow the excess fabric to be pulled gently into the walking foot. The foot will ease out any fullness so there are no gathers, tucks, or pleats in the fabric. Gently walk your fingers just in front of the walking foot for the entire length of the seam.

NOTE: *If you have starched the fabric, it will seldom—if ever—push and accumulate in front of the foot. You'll be able to rest your hands gently to the side of the foot, and simply guide the fabric.*

Stretching the seam in front of and behind the foot to prevent tucks only distorts the finished quilt. When the batting is stretched and then stitched, it will try to rebound to its original shape, causing dips and valleys at the cross seams and fluting at the edges. You'll be creating a waffle!

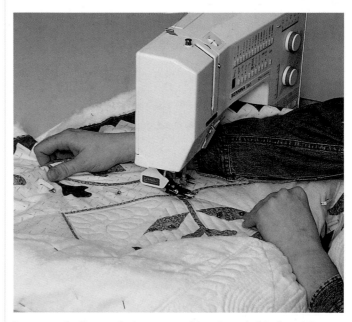

Incorrect feeding technique: stretching from behind and front

If you follow the guidelines for preparation (that is, starch and good pressing) and for feeding excess fullness, the quilt will finish flat and square without tucks or distortion. Allow the walking foot to work for you. This is why you bought it.

Tip

If Your Walking Foot Balks at Seams

Sometimes the walking foot gets hung up on bulky seam allowances. If this happens, you will see a few tiny stitches in that area. Stop, lift the foot slightly, and set it down again to release the fabric snagged under the foot. If this happens often, you can modify the foot as described on page 29-30.

If you experience problems watching the needle, adjust the height of your chair. Retrain your eyes to watch the needle and know where it is going with every stitch. If you watch the foot and compensate for the position of the foot in relation to the seam, the needle will not be where it needs to be. If you watch the needle, you have the control to adjust the seam to accommodate the needle's position. Raising the height of your chair also eliminates glare from the machine light and allows you to see the hole where the needle is stitching.

As you approach the last $1/4$" of the seam, stop and decrease the stitch length on the machine to $1/2$ or .5. Be sure that the last $1/4$" of the seam is stitched with very tiny stitches (50 stitches to the inch) to lock off the end of the stitching. If you reach the edge and realize that you forgot to lock off, you can take tiny backstitches. Do this before you cut the threads.

Tip

When locking off, always cut the top thread first. You can cut the top threads as you move from one area of the quilt to another. Always clip as close as possible to the fabric. When you remove the quilt from under the machine, turn it over and clip the bobbin threads on the back. A light tug on the bobbin thread will pull any top tail through the layers and secure it in the batting. Clip the bobbin thread as close as possible as well.

Now go back and examine the seam for quality and proper technique. Use this checklist to focus on any trouble spots you need to work on.

▣ Stitching should be on the low side of the ditch at all times, with no stitches on the fold of the high side.

▣ Stitches should be consistent in length.

▣ There should be no gathers, tucks, or stretched areas along seams or at intersections on the top of the quilt. (Problems here can indicate that the seam was not pressed and starched, the quilt was not layered adequately, the foot is not feeding properly, or you are not using your fingers properly to feed the fabric to the foot.)

▣ There should be no tucks or puckers on the back of the quilt. (Tucks and puckers are caused by poor layering techniques.)

▣ Stitches should be locked off adequately at the beginning and end of every seam. (If you forget to do this, the binding will not secure the stitches.)

▣ The area where seams cross should be exactly perpendicular and square. (If the line sags below a straight line, you've allowed the fabric to push ahead, and the finished quilt will look distorted.)

▣ No bobbin thread should show on the top of the quilt. (A problem here results from improper tension.)

▣ When you look for the stitching, you should see nothing. Good ditch quilting is totally invisible. (If you see stitches, determine if it results from guiding problems or using too large a needle.)

Each of these small details needs attention if you want to master machine quilting. I stress: it is essential that you work out the potential problems *before* quilting the actual quilt. If you have problems with the sample block, go back and adjust the machine and practice the feeding technique until you are prepared to tackle the quilt. Better to do this now then to be picking out stitches on your quilt.

Straight-Line Quilting: *Lines and Grids*

 hen you take straight-line quilting out of the ditch, you can get incredible effects on the surface of the quilt! If you look at and study antique quilts, you will be surprised at the amount of straight-line quilting and the marvelous effects created with this basically very simple technique. Read on to discover all you can do with your machine using only a walking foot!

Channel Quilting

Parallel rows of quilted lines, or channel quilting, is common on many antique quilts. Lines of quilting can be as close together as $^1/_4$" or as far apart as you want. Channels can run lengthwise, crosswise, or diagonally. The simplicity of this style of quilting can be striking when used as background for a complex quilted-feather or appliqué design.

Channel quilting

Grid Quilting

Grid quilting is another common form of machine-guided quilting done with a walking foot. Grids can be straight, diagonal, double diagonal, hanging diamonds, plaids, or any combination you choose to achieve a particular effect. This style of quilting adds surface texture to a quilt top with a strong pieced or appliqué design without introducing conflicting pattern. It can appear over the entire surface of the quilt, in the background of a block, around a design, or within the design itself.

Grid quilting inside and around the outside of design

Grid quilting is functional quilting that also adds a wonderful relief to the overall surface. It often appears on antique quilts as it hand quilts quickly. It makes an excellent choice for quilting on busy fabric: straight lines show up nicely and provide a pleasing contrast.

Strong and durable, grid quilting is a marvelous way to do extensive, close machine quilting on quilts such as Log Cabin, Pineapple, and other old, traditional patterns. You don't have to practice for hours to produce heavy, beautiful quilting if you choose straight-line designs to enhance your quilt tops.

Variety of background line quilting patterns

MARKING LINES AND GRIDS

If you mark the lines on the quilt top and work with a walking foot, the quilting will be very accurate. The foot enables you to stitch straight lines and keep them parallel. There is a wide variety of precut grid and diamond stencils in various sizes available to make marking fairly easy. These are a fine alternative to marking with a ruler, which can be tedious and inaccurate if you aren't careful.

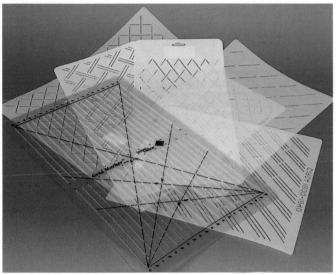

Variety of grid stencils

If you choose to mark grids with a ruler, it is best to measure along the outside edge of the block or quilt. Measure the finished sides of the block or quilt, and then divide the length of each side by the size of the grid. Choose a grid that is evenly divisible into the length of the side. For example, an 18" square could have a $1/2$", 1", or $1\,1/2$" grid, as these numbers divide evenly into eighteen. Place dots along the edges of the area to be gridded to mark the desired distance between the grid lines. Connect the dots to establish the line. This method is far more accurate than using a ruler to mark from previously drawn lines—a method that quickly compounds even the slightest error.

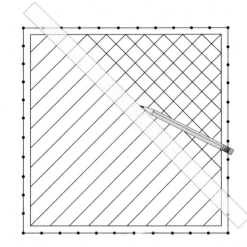

Marking and connecting dots to create grid

Diagonal-Grid Spacing	
Desired Grid Size	Interval Between Dots
$3/8$" grid	$1/2$"
$1/2$" grid	$3/4$"
$3/4$" grid	1"
$7/8$" grid	$1\,1/4$"
1"+ grid	$1\,1/2$"

An excellent tool for marking lines and grids is the Grid Marker by June Tailor, Inc. It is made from stencil plastic and cut with 17"-long lines, $1/2$" apart. There are 60°, 45°, and 30° lines printed over the slits for diagonal placement, as well as registration marks for drawing crosswise lines for grids.

Some walking feet come with a guide bar that enables you to avoid marking every quilting line. You need a foot that comes with two bars: one for the right and one for the left of the foot. The left bar is used to stitch to the right of a line; vice versa for the right bar. These bars are designed to ride on top of a previously stitched line. Determine the distance you want between the lines, and set the guide bar to that measurement. The guide bar runs on top of the previously stitched line to help with the next line of stitching.

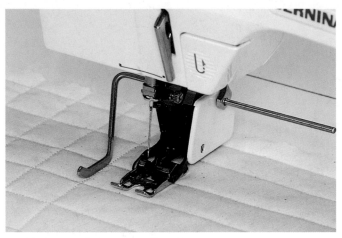

Guide bar used to measure line distance

Tip

Tip for Using Guide Bars

If you plan to use a guide bar, stiffly starch the fabric you are quilting. I can tell you from experience that you can't watch both the guide bar and how the foot is feeding the fabric at the same time. It is easy for the fabric to move ahead of the foot if you are not feeding it properly, but you have to watch to do this. If you are monitoring the feeding, you are not looking at the guide bar to stay on the line accurately.

If the lines are spaced closely enough, the edge of the foot can provide a good guide. You can watch both the foot and the fabric feeding up to the foot at the same time.

Heavy straight-line work stitched on the bias can result in slight "pulling" of the fabric between the stitched lines. Because I prefer the look of cotton batting and the puckering from shrinkage, this pulling is camouflaged, and can even enhance that "old" look. If you prefer, you can eliminate this pulling with a darning foot and free-motion techniques, but your free-motion skills must be excellent. This is not my method of choice, especially if the lines extend across the entire quilt.

Example of pulling between quilting lines

When stitching triple lines, I find that if I stitch the center line of all the sets first, then go back and stitch on either side, there is minimal—if any—pulling.

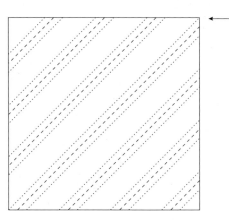

Practice Stitching

For practice and as a permanent record of different types of straight-line work, I made samples of every design in the illustration on page 112. I find these samples helpful when I'm deciding on a size or look for a grid pattern.

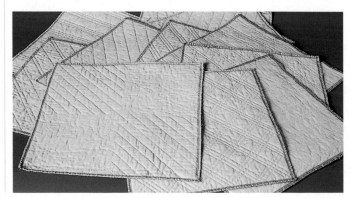

Sample grid-quilted blocks

AN EARLY MACHINE QUILTER

Ernest B. Haight was one of the forefathers of early machine piecing and quilting. He started piecing quilt tops on the machine in the 1930s, and is considered by many to be partially responsible for the quick-pieced, sheeted-triangle technique popular today. He followed his piecing success with machine quilting a few years later. His son estimated that he made over 300 quilts, and he was a consistent ribbon-winner with his machine quilted quilts.

Ernest Haight was a master of grid quilting and developed a system for continuously quilting grids. Every time he reached the edge of the quilt, he'd make a 90° turn. The illustration below shows the "route" of the quilting lines. Notice that there are several starts and stops to get all the lines quilted. The benefit of this method is that the bulk of the quilt is always to the left, except when stitching the two long, center lines.

As you study the illustration, you'll notice that each segment mirrors one from the opposite end. You start on the top left corner of the quilt, and then rotate and stitch the second line, starting from the bottom right corner. When turned, this becomes the top left corner. All starting points then move down a long side of the quilt, alternating sides. Although it involves a lot of turning and repackaging, this method is worth a try, especially on smaller quilts.

HANGING DIAMONDS

Log Cabins and many other quilt designs are so busy both in design and fabric that fancy quilting is lost. A traditional way to achieve heavy quilting with straight lines—yet add diagonal lines for interest— is a method called "hanging diamonds." This technique uses straight lines, parallel to the border, for the lengthwise direction of the quilt, and then crosses the stitches with one-directional diagonal lines.

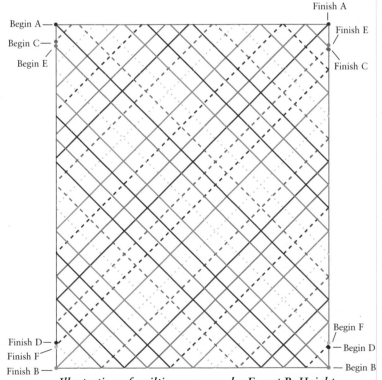

Illustration of quilting sequence by Ernest B. Haight

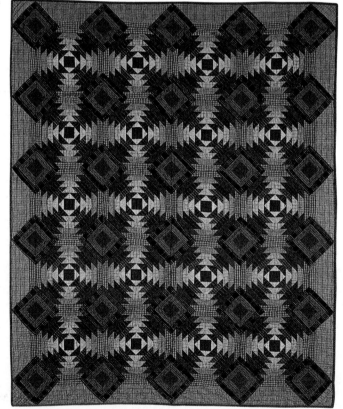

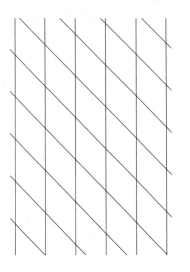

Hanging-diamond grid

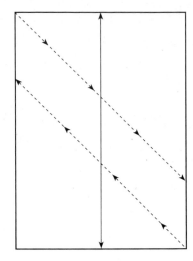

Diagonal anchoring for a rectangular quilt

Package the quilt so that you can anchor the lengthwise center seam first. Next, anchor the diagonal direction so you will have anchor lines to cross as you quilt. If the quilt is square, this diagonal line will run from corner to corner.

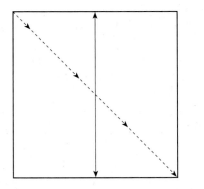

Diagonal anchoring for square quilt

If the quilt is longer than it is wide, run two anchor lines diagonally, each one anchoring a different corner.

Repackage the quilt so that you can quilt all lengthwise lines to the right of the center, top to bottom. Flip the quilt around, repackage, and quilt the lines from the right of the center, top to bottom. Now package the quilt diagonally, so that you are working from the center of the quilt out toward the corner. Flip the quilt around and repackage so that you are repeating the process on the other half, working out to the corner. Throw these diagonal packages over your left shoulder to make them easier to work with.

Generally, this type of quilting extends into the border, so all that is left to do is trim, square, and bind. It gets easier all the time!

Tip

Final Thought

Once you've mastered quilting straight lines, I encourage you to move on to Chapters 11 and 12 to learn free-motion techniques. You will be able to quilt short, straight lines much more quickly and easily. You can stitch without maneuvering or turning the quilt under the sewing machine to change sewing directions.

Free-Motion Quilting: *Basics*

CHAPTER 11

Free-motion quilting will open up a whole new world to you. I have no doubt that it will become your favorite method of machine quilting. You'll need to practice to master free-motion quilting, and be willing to experiment with samples, but you will find the time well spent when you are able to reproduce beautiful quilting designs in minutes. Removing the presser foot allows you incredible freedom! You can stitch forward, backward, side-to-side, in circles—anywhere you want to go—without ever turning the quilt. With practice and perseverance, *you can do it!*

My approach to free-motion quilting is a bit different than most. I believe one of the most important factors in learning to machine quilt is preparation. I can't emphasize enough the importance of preparing a suitable work space, choosing good equipment, and understanding the workings of your machine, needles, and thread. So…be sure you've read the first eight chapters before you dive into free-motion quilting. You'll be finishing up that stack of unfinished tops before you know it.

Many beginners are taught to stipple quilt before they are taught any other machine-quilting technique. I think this is a backwards way to learn. Stippling is a more advanced technique that involves quilting *small curves* forward, backward, sideways, and every other direction. If you can't quilt in every direction with some control, you are not likely to be successful.

The process of learning to free-motion quilt is progressive —the steps are building blocks. In this chapter, you will start with a foundation of basic skills. You will learn to manipulate and control the movement of the quilt manually under a sewing machine needle. Take your time and work through the following exercises. You will gradually build on the skills you master to move to the next level.

Practicing Free-Motion Technique

As a teacher, my biggest delight in the classroom comes when a student says, "I love this! It is so much fun!" All tension, doubt, and concern about perfection is gone. This is true freedom with a sewing machine.

The reality is this: free-motion quilting is not instant gratification. It takes many hours of practice to master the techniques. That doesn't mean, however, that you can't complete many projects as you learn. My suggestion is to put perfectionism under the bed for awhile, if not forever, and just enjoy the process. If you become self critical and look for all the mistakes, it will be hard to invest the time it takes to become proficient. Very few (if any) machine quilters are "perfect" quilters. Even the top award-winning machine quilters can point out their glitches! Your abilities are relative to the time you put into learning a skill, and your expectations should be realistic in accordance with time expended. Remember, you are not being judged or graded! Okay: enough of my pep talk (or, as some might say, soap box). Let's have fun learning to free-motion quilt.

Laying the Foundation

Before you begin practicing the designs, think about and plan the motion necessary to create the patterns. Consider your sewing machine an extension of your arms and eyes. The machine must become a part of you, not an obstacle in your way. If you haven't cleaned and waxed the sewing surface of the machine, do so now to keep the fabric gliding smoothly through the machine. If you have prewashed your fabrics, treat them with starch to restore a crisp finish. This will also increase your ease in moving the fabric through the machine.

Quilting Aids

In free-motion quilting, your hands control the movement of the quilt under the needle. There are a few tools and gadgets you might want to try; many beginners find that these aids really help them gain better control of the fabric. The photo below shows a sampling of some of these products: rubber filing fingers, quilter's gloves (three styles), latex finger gloves, Sortkwik Finger Moistener, and machine-quilting hoops. Fellow machine-quilter Diane Gaudynski introduced me to Neutrogena Norwegian Formula Body Emulsion, a non-greasy hand lotion. This particular lotion leaves your fingers slightly tacky and allows you to get a good grip without covering your fingertips. When you are quilting very small areas with tiny stitches, or working a very detailed design, the nerve endings in your fingertips can really help with the control of the fabric.

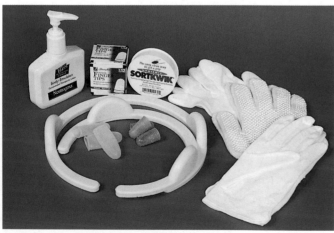

Variety of quilting aids

When I work on large quilts with designs requiring quite a bit of movement of the layers, I wear rubber filing fingers on the first three fingers of each hand and on each thumb. The rubber grip allows me to move the fabric with a lot less hand pressure and with less stress to my shoulders and neck. You can purchase rubber filing fingers at an office supply store. They have tiny tentacles on the surface that really grab the fabric. They come in various sizes, so try them on each finger for fit.

If my hands and wrists start to get fatigued, I turn to gloves. Gloves do get a bit warm, but they enable me to work by placing the palms of my hands lightly on the quilt, giving me more surface to work with and a bit more power than just my fingertips. When I quilt very small areas with very small stitches, I use Sortkwik or lotion. Experiment and find your magic gadget or notion.

The First Steps

To begin the stitching process, put the darning foot on your machine, replace the throat plate with the straight-stitch plate, and drop or cover your feed dogs (whichever your machine requires). Check your manual for guidance if necessary. Because the feed dogs are dropped, you don't need to adjust the stitch length. You control the stitch length by the speed in which you move the fabric in relation to the speed of the machine motor.

Tip

Some machine mechanics recommend setting the stitch length on zero to take away the working action of the feed dogs, saying this puts less wear and tear on the machine parts.

MACHINE SPEED

If you have ever taken a machine quilting class, you have probably heard someone say that the faster you run the machine, the easier it is to quilt. Essentially this is true—it is easier to get a good rhythm when the needle is moving quickly. However, if you aren't breathing because you are scared to death you will run over your fingers, you aren't going to think "fast" is easy! To control the machine speed, you must have total control of the foot pedal. It may be tempting to use built-in motor speed functions. I don't recommend this. I want you to learn to make the machine adapt to your needs, rather than you adapting to the machine. To begin, run the machine at all the various speeds you can create with the foot pedal, and learn to listen to the motor speed. Eventually, you will develop a very close relationship with your machine. You'll hear any changes in the sound of the motor and adjust your foot pressure almost instantaneously. In a way, this is similar to the challenge of walking, chewing gum, patting your head, and rubbing your tummy. You might say you can't do it, but you can if you practice.

Tip

Quilting Barefoot

If you've never sewn without shoes, try it. When you remove your shoes, your foot can feel every change of pressure to the foot pedal, and you'll have much more control of the machine speed. If you must wear shoes, the thicker the sole, the less feeling and control you'll have. Running and tennis shoes are the least suitable.

Think of machine quilting as dancing with your machine. If you were on the dance floor dancing to the waltz, and suddenly the music changed to the rumba, chances are you would stumble just a bit, stop to listen to the rhythm of the new music, remember the steps, tell you feet what to do, and then start the new dance. The same process occurs when the speed of your machine changes. Stitch length is directly related to the speed the needle moves in and out of the fabric. If the machine speed changes,

you must hear it, determine if it is faster or slower, and then tell your hands if they need to slow down or speed up to compensate.

Layer a few sample practice blocks using two pieces of muslin and 100-percent cotton batting. The cotton layers stick together, so don't bother to pin. You won't need to dodge pins or stop to remove them. Instead you can concentrate on learning to coordinate your hands, eyes, ears, and foot.

Starting with both the top and bobbin threads on top of the quilt prevents the threads from jamming and snarling on the underside. Make it a habit to always bring the bobbin thread to the surface of the fabric before beginning to stitch. To do this, lower the presser bar, hold the top thread on top of the foot, and take one complete stitch. As you hold the top thread, the bobbin thread will pop up into the hole of the foot as the stitch is completed.

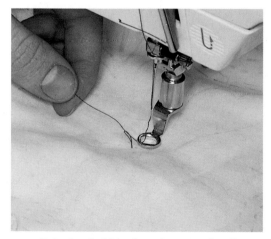

Bringing bobbin thread to top of quilt

Lift the presser bar, move the fabric to the left and pull the bobbin thread through the fabric. This action also pulls the top thread down through the hole of the darning foot. Hold both threads and realign the needle with the hole the threads emerge from. Lower the needle and the presser foot.

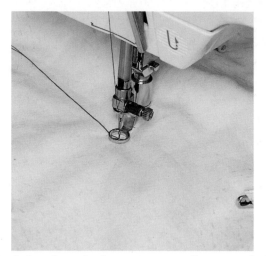

Both threads under foot; reinsert needle in same hole

Hold the threads snugly to the side and start to run your machine. You'll need to move the fabric manually because you've disengaged the feeding system. This is where the concept "hand quilting with an electric needle" comes into play. Don't worry about locking off or what you are going to quilt. You'll just be scribbling for a while.

Start out with your foot barely pressing on the foot control. Make the machine go as slowly as it can go. Gradually start to speed up, going faster, then faster. Move the fabric as best you can, but don't worry about what you are stitching. You may feel yourself begin to tense up a bit as the machine goes faster and faster. Become aware of your comfort level and stay at that speed for a while. Breathe!

Once you get to a comfortable speed, stay there. Uneven foot pressure causes erratic bursts of speed, and the machine will speed up, slow down, and speed up again. Learning to keep the motor steady, at one constant speed, is the biggest secret to controlling stitch quality. Once you can keep the speed static, you can start learning to control your hands. Train your ear to monitor the motor sound constantly, and it will take over the job of keeping your foot in control. You won't have to continually think about it. *Relax* and breathe!

Tip

Regulating Speed

If you find it hard to keep a constant speed with your foot control, consider placing a little block of wood on the back of the pedal. Once you've reached your optimum speed, the block prevents any further changes.

If you just can't get it all to work together, now is the time to try one your machine's built-in motor speeds. Setting the machine to half speed and pushing the foot control all the way to the floor often gives you just the right speed to start with and keeps you from constantly changing speed. Once you get the feel for this consistency, go back and try to control the speed with your foot instead of relying on the machine's computer.

HAND SPEED

Once you find a comfortable motor speed and can keep it constant, it is time to start coordinating your hands to that speed. You want to develop a rhythm with your hands and the motor speed of the machine. To do this, think about dancing again. If you had your heart set on dancing the rumba, but the orchestra only played waltzes, you would have a difficult time dancing rumba steps while your ear was hearing waltz rhythm. Keeping in synchronization is key to good quality quilting. If the machine is speeding ahead, and your hands are moving very slowly or erratically, your stitches will be tiny and cluttered. If the machine is running very slowly, and your hands want to go faster, the stitches will be very long and angular. If you are running the machine at erratic speeds, gunning and slowing down constantly, your hands cannot react to the speed changes instantly, so the stitches will always be out of control and uneven. You want a steady, flowing motion of the fabric, with the machine running at a constant speed. Dance to the sound of your machine.

Eventually, for the majority of your quilting, you will want your free-motion stitches to match any stitches made with the walking foot. If you ditch or grid quilt part of the quilt and finish up with free-motion work, your goal is to make all of the stitches the same length. This is where practice pays off. Take a breath and relax! You are drawing with the needle.

In learning to control your hands, you will be training your eyes to control your hand speed. Become aware of how fast your hands must move the fabric under the needle to create the stitch length you want. If the stitches appear too long, slow down your hands, not the machine. If they are too short, speed up your hands, not the machine. The machine stays the same, your hands compensate.

Once you get a feel for the motion, start to move the fabric very slowly, side to side, keeping the machine at your favorite speed. Check the stitch length; the stitches should be very short and close together. Begin to speed up the motion of your hands, while keeping the machine speed constant. The stitch length should get longer and longer until eventually you are creating a basting stitch and your sample resembles the example below. This demonstrates how the stitch length is controlled totally by the motion of your hands as you maintain a consistent speed on your machine.

Refine the stitch length to the *exact length* you preferred when you were using the walking foot. What you are doing here is measuring the length of your stitches with your eyes *as you make them*. If the stitches are too long, slow down your hands or speed up the machine, keeping it consistently at the new speed. If the stitches are too short, speed up your hands or slow down the machine. Remember: you are dancing with your machine, and rhythm is critical.

Stitch-length variations

Tip

As you continue to make progress, you'll learn that stitch length is also affected by the shape and size of the piece you are quilting. Large designs quilted within a block might look best stitched with an average-length stitch. Stipple quilting around a larger design might dictate very short, tiny stitches. Often the technique determines the stitch length as well.

Bringing It All Together

HAND POSITION AND MOVEMENT

Remember: when you are free-motion quilting, you never turn the fabric, but glide it where you want it to go. Keep your hands relaxed and your wrists arched up slightly. Quilt with your fingertips, not your whole hand. The position is similar to playing the piano or reaching down to grab an orange. The more you rest your hand flat on the fabric, the more resistance you'll find as you try to move the fabric.

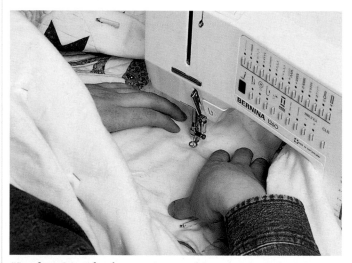

Hand position for free-motion work

Use a gentle, sliding motion as you quilt. Too much pressure causes the fabric to drag, stutter, and jerk. Rather than holding your arms up or out to your sides, rest them on the edge of the table or on the quilt as it lays on the table. This enables you to lean into the work, removing the tension from your shoulders and back. A good chair and good posture is critical.

Try these exercises to help develop your skills. Stitch forward and backward as shown below. Don't worry if your stitches are uneven. For now, concern yourself with the directional movement of the fabric only. At first you might find that you are comfortable going in one direction, but feel awkward stitching in the opposite direction. Keep practicing this exercise until you are comfortable moving the fabric in both directions, and then practice making all the stitches the same length.

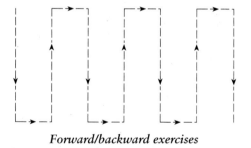

Forward/backward exercises

Next, practice stitching side-to-side: left to right, and back again. This will probably feel foreign to you, as you generally don't sew sideways. Practice until it is just as easy to go right as left. When you've mastered the motion, aim for stitches the same size as those in the previous forward/backward exercise.

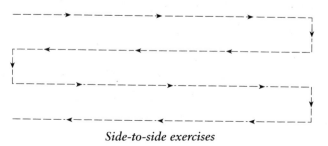

Side-to-side exercises

LOCKING OFF THREAD TAILS

You'll need to lock off the threads at the beginning and end of each line of stitching as you free-motion quilt.

To lock off the stitches, slow the speed of the fabric, *not* the machine. Your goal is to make very tiny stitches (for between $1/8$" and $1/4$") at the beginning and end of every line—the same as with ditch quilting. It will take practice to become accustomed to using different hand speeds while the machine is running at a constant speed. You'll need total control of both your hands and your foot control.

When beginning a line of stitching, *start* with the machine at your preferred fastest speed. Move your hands very slowly, forming the tiny stitches. Then speed up your hands until you've regained the speed you need to make the stitches the desired length. To end a line of quilting, slow your hands, but not your machine. Once you've made the necessary tiny stitches, stop the machine *instantly*—on a dime. If you allow the machine to slow down or speed up gradually, the stitch length will be affected. Practice stitching the following lines shown at top of the next page until you have mastered the locking stitches.

Lock
stitch

Zigzag side-to-side

CURVES

Practice stitching curves next. Try drawing "e" and "l" shapes as though practicing penmanship. Keep practicing until the curves are smooth, with no points or ragged edges. Stitch loops, circles, and anything else "curvy" that comes to mind. Aim to keep all the stitches the same size. Avoid the tendency to stitch slowly up one side of the loop and pick up speed on the down side. Control will give you nice, consistent stitches.

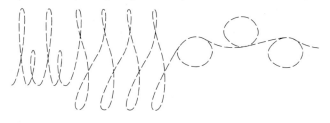

Free-motion curves

Continue practicing by drawing stars, hearts, your name, pictures, and so on. Do not draw these images on the fabric; rather, visualize them and use your hands to reproduce what your mind sees. It often helps to draw the shapes on paper before stitching the design on fabric.

Another way to practice is to stitch on fabrics with large-scale prints. Quilt around the print motifs for practice. The freedom you'll experience working with a darning foot is like flying! You can go anywhere.

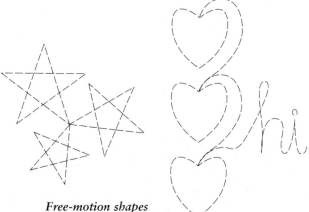

Free-motion shapes

Practice sample

Tip

You are probably discovering that no one speed suits every task. You'll adjust machine speed depending upon the complexity, size, and shape of the design you are quilting, as well as the size of the quilt.

There are all sorts of designs that you can quilt into a background area without ever marking a line. Practice quilting random patterns and shapes with a quilt sandwich made of two large pieces of fabric, such as muslin, and cotton batting. Make your practice piece about the size of a lap or small crib quilt. Pin the layers together, and start to quilt the space free-style. The larger piece gives you experience dealing with some bulk under the machine arm: you'll need to roll it to fit and manage while stitching. Remember: guide, don't turn the quilt, and avoid looking at only the needle. Get used to roaming the entire immediate area in *anticipation* of where you'll be moving next.

As you learn and begin to practice all you must to achieve good stitches, let me share some information from a study done on how the brain learns physical skills.

It can take our brain up to six uninterrupted hours to learn one new physical skill. If the learning process is interrupted, it might take even longer. This means that each technique described in this chapter could—potentially—take six hours to master. I have never seen it take that long; generally, a student is on her way in a few hours. Her technique may not be perfect, but it is certainly passable.

In today's world of instant gratification, it might sound inconceivable to spend that much time to learn to quilt, but do you remember how much time it took to learn to play a musical instrument? To ride a bicycle? To stand up and move on roller skates? When we were young we were willing to practice as long as it took so we could do it! As adults, we want to be able to do it now. Be patient. Once you get these foundation skills under your belt, you will gain the confidence you need to want to keep going. On the other hand, if you don't learn these basic skills, the next step—staying on design lines—will really put you off.

Bottom line? Don't skip this necessary step. It will pay off huge dividends! If you spend just ten minutes a day for six months, practicing and quilting small projects, you will become a very good quilter in that short amount of time. If you spend ten minutes every six months, it just isn't going to happen.

Troubleshooting Common Problems

Problem: Machine needles break.

Causes/Solutions:

◘ Your rhythm is off. The quilt is moving too fast for the speed of the needle.

◘ The top thread may be wrapped around a spool pin, cone-holder rod, thread guide, or take-up lever. The excess stress on the thread usually snaps the needle before the thread breaks. (You are likely to hear this before it happens; the machine will emit a "pinging" sound.) Check the threading and rethread if necessary.

◘ The needle is too small for your skill level, or the thread you are using. Try a larger-size needle.

◘ The needle is not inserted correctly into the needle bar. Check to make sure it is inserted properly, as far up as it will go.

Problem: Uneven stitches.

Causes/Solutions:

◘ Your machine bed is sticky, making it hard for you to glide the fabric. Clean the machine bed with rubbing alcohol, and then wax and buff the surface smooth.

◘ Your prewashed fabric is dragging against the machine bed. Try starching the fabric.

◘ Your machine speed or hand speed is erratic. Be sure to maintain a consistent machine speed, and practice smooth and even hand movements.

◘ You may be sitting too low to your machine for proper eye/hand coordination.

◘ Your machine is too far away for you to have steady control of the quilt.

◘ Your fingers have no grip, so you are pressing down on the fabric to move it, which creates more resistance.

◘ Your darning foot rides too low on the quilt and gets hung-up on high areas. Lower the presser-bar tension or use the large quilting foot on your machine.

◘ Your concentration is wandering. Refocus or take a break.

◘ Remember-if you quit today—tomorrow would have been the day you "got it".

Free-Motion Quilting: *Beyond Basics*

CHAPTER 12

Once you are comfortable with the free-motion techniques described in the previous chapter, and you have gained control of the quilt layers, the bulk, and stitch consistency, you are ready to move on to the next step: design lines.

Borders, connector blocks, and large open spaces in the quilt design are perfect places to show off decorative quilting. Free-motion quilting gives you the maneuverability necessary to reproduce the intricate designs used by hand quilters. Almost any hand-quilting design can be duplicated using free-motion methods, once you have honed your skills. Free-motion quilting gives you access to small designs, sharp curves, and intricate patterns that are next to impossible to achieve with a presser foot. After practicing and experimenting, you'll find yourself using your darning foot to ditch quilt shorter lines and accomplish many other designs you never dreamed you could do.

As you first attempt quilting on a drawn line, don't be surprised if you think you need to go back to square one. Your early attempts may feel like "three steps forward, two steps back!" Hang in there: you have the basic skills you need. You are simply adding more difficult techniques, requiring you to focus on more than just moving the fabric and keeping the stitches even. This is why I was so adamant that you practice the foundation exercises in the previous chapter. The foundation skills you gained there will carry you through this next level.

Study the designs in the back of the book (pages 158-170). Find the star on each design, and finger-trace around the design, following the numbers. Trace the design several times until you become familiar with the "road" the needle will take. Quilting this line will be much like driving a very curvy road for the first time. You will be tempted to slow down at every curve to figure out where to go next. If you already know the road by finger-tracing it a few times, you'll be more apt to stay on the line and keep your speed steady.

Now, rather than watching the needle as you did for ditch quilting, you must train your eyes not to look at the needle or in the opening of the foot to stay on a line. To help you make this transition, imagine you are driving a car. You back out of the driveway, and as you start forward, you stare only at the hood ornament. If you don't look down the road, and keep staring at the hood ornament, you'll be out of control and flying blind. Now translate this to quilting. If you only stare at the needle, and not the line ahead of you, you have no idea of where the line goes and what you need to do to get the line and the needle in the same place. You need to know where you are going to get there successfully. Finger-tracing the design helps you know your "road." As you draw designs onto the quilt top, try to draw them in the exact order you will stitch them. This reenforces the road map. As you stitch, keep your eyes ahead of the needle, just as you do while driving, so you know what to expect and can prepare your hands to make it happen. You need to look ahead, look behind (as you do with the rear-view mirror), and be aware of where you are, all at the same time. This will immediately improve your workmanship and control.

Getting Started

1. Bring the bobbin thread up, hold onto both threads, and place the needle at the beginning of the design line. Lock off the stitches.

Tip

When clipping the thread tails at the beginning of a line of quilting, stretch the threads taut and clip them as close to the fabric as possible. The tails will relax and disappear completely into the batting. At the end of a quilting line, you can often pull on the top thread until a bubble of bobbin thread appears, enabling you to clip both at the same time. A pair of small, sharp, curved blade snips are really helpful for this. The thinner the blade, the closer you will clip the tails.

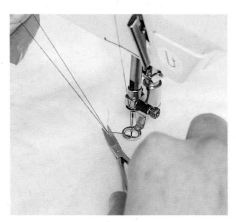

Cut thread tails close to quilt surface with curved-blade thread snips.

2. Trace the design lines with your eyes to get used to the view from your seated position. If necessary, adjust the light source to enhance the line drawn on the fabric surface. Remember: the secret of staying on the line is not to look at the needle or in the hole of the darning foot, but to keep your eyes slightly ahead of the needle.

Tip

Small Is Better

Use the smallest darning foot available for your machine so as not obstruct your view of the line. A large foot covers the line where you need to see. A small foot almost disappears from your range of vision, allowing you to see ahead. It also allows you to glance back and check that the needle is on the line.

PRACTICE STITCHING

Remember the driving analogy? Quilt the way you drive. Know where you are going before you get there. Check on what you are doing at the needle, and continually glance back and forth. Once you can do this, you'll be able to stay on the line and keep your stitches even. Let's work through some examples.

Tip

Focus

Learning to machine quilt on the lines takes a lot of concentration. Give yourself plenty of uninterrupted, quiet time to practice, and don't expect to quilt perfectly for a while.

The designs on page 158 correspond with the steps below. Use them in your practice sessions, repeating them over and over until the concepts are assimilated and there are no longer any stumbling blocks.

Loops: The stencil pattern illustrated below involves lots of loops. When machine quilted, the lines should connect in the center, eliminating the need to start and stop, and creating a continuous design. The original stencil gives no mark to indicate the meeting point. If you were hand quilting this design, you would go through the layers to get from one loop to another. You can't do this on the machine. You'll need to stitch through the center three times, hitting the same spot each time. To do this, put a dot in the center of the design. As you stitch the loops, look at the dot before you reach it. If you look at the needle or in the hole of the foot, you'll only see where you are at that moment. If the line curves, the momentum of your hands will take you past the curve before you can react and follow the line accurately. If you read the line ahead, you are ready to go around the curve because you know where it is before you get to it. Once you know you'll hit the dot, you can move your eyes to the line ahead.

Dot system for guidance

Tip

Think Ahead

The key concept to remember with this technique is *anticipation*. *Anticipate* where you need to be next. Don't worry where you are right now; you've already thought about that.

The next design is not continuous. Each "brush stroke" is separate. You can make the strokes continuous by connecting them as shown. Quilt the bottom half last. Specific instructions follow.

Making a design continuous

Look ahead and plan for the stops in the design. Go over the top of the first unit and continue on until the needle reaches the line of the second unit. Just as the needle touches the second line, stop and make a couple of stitches in that spot. You might want to draw lines that elongate the tails to connect the design; then you can look ahead and won't have to guess at their position.

Once again, look ahead and stitch the underside of the first unit until the imaginary line of the second unit stops you. Begin stitching the top line of the second unit. Aim the needle into the same needle hole that you made when you stopped for this line before. Think of it as a dot, similar to the one in the previous illustration. Repeat the process with the top of all the units.

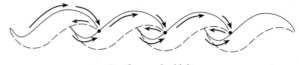

Quilt top half first.

Now stitch the bottom line of all the units, looking ahead to identify the needle holes you'll need to hit to accurately close the design.

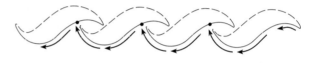

Finish with bottom half.

Tip

You can also quilt these patterns in a top-to-bottom motion instead of side-to-side. The decision depends on your personal preference, as well as how you package the quilt.

Points and Corners: These always seem hard for a beginner, but there is an easy way to approach them. To create a point or a corner, allow the needle to stay in one place for just a second to make a couple of stitches in the same hole. If you stay in the hole too long, the bobbin thread tends to come up into the hole and cause an unsightly knot.

Practice stitching straight lines with the pattern on the next page. Allow your eyes to jump from one point to the next, instead of following the line. Look ahead to where you need to be, and your hands will take you straight there. If you follow the line with your eye, or look inside the darning foot, you will tend to wobble the lines as you stitch.

Stop for a heartbeat at every dot.

Adding lines or other marks can make you more accurate when stitching any design. It may be dots, arrows, or a solid line without any bridges.

Starting and Stopping: If you need to reposition your hands as you work through a design, stop with the needle in the down position. This prevents the quilt from sliding and causing a loop of excess thread on the back.

When working with a design that requires you to go from one area to another, do not cut the thread. Lock the threads at the end of the first unit, pull them across the quilt top, lock them again at the beginning of the new line, and resume stitching. After you finish with the design, clip all the connecting threads.

> *Tip*
>
> If you are quilting with nylon thread, clip the thread on the top of the quilt as soon as you pass the lock-off area. Because the nylon blends in completely with the fabric, you can easily miss these dragged threads, only to snag up on them later.

QUILTING THE PRACTICE QUILT

By now you are probably bored to tears with practicing. Once you are able to stay fairly close to the lines of your practice designs, I suggest you start to quilt real projects. Go to your closet and look at the pile. Chances are the quilt tops at the bottom are no longer your very favorites. You might even wonder why you made them in the first place! Quilt tops like these are perfect candidates for your first quilting attempts. Layer one of these tops with cotton batting—preferably one that will shrink a bit—and a busy backing fabric. This is a good time to shop the sale tables at the quilt shop. Choose fabrics with busy patterns, in colors that coordinate with your quilt tops.

It is important to get your speed and rhythm in order, so warm up before starting on your quilt. Stitching a sample block not only tells you which threads you prefer and if you need to adjust the tension on your machine, but it also gives you the opportunity to warm up and practice the designs you have chosen.

I sometimes discover while I am warming up that it just isn't going to be a quilting day. I can't get my coordination together, and I get irritable and frustrated. This is not a good state of mind for tackling a quilt. It's time to garden instead.

Keep the designs simple, small, and curvy at this point. One of the greatest pitfalls to developing good skills is jumping into a design too difficult for your skill level. Draw the chosen design several times onto a practice piece and quilt it over and over again. This repetitive motion trains your eyes and hands how to quilt the pattern and stay on the line accurately. This is *practicing with a purpose!* You may not yet be able to quilt every design you desire, but you have learned how to quilt this one well.

More Advanced Techniques

CONTINUOUS-CURVE QUILTING

Continuous-curve quilting is another form of free-motion quilting. I discovered this method in 1980 in Barbara Johannah's book *Continuous-Curve Quilting*. (See page 175.) I could hardly contain my excitement over the possibilities this offered for the quilts I was making at the time. Barbara's method achieves the look of outline quilting without the starting, stopping, and turning of the quilt traditionally necessary to achieve straight lines 1/4" from the seam. Instead, gentle arcs replace the straight lines and corners. The arcs go through the corners to reach the next area to be quilted, reducing the number of starts and stops to almost none.

The stitched arcs are contained within each unit, going corner to corner, with the deepest point $1/4''$ from the seam at the midpoint. This technique gives wonderful dimension to the surface of pieced blocks. The main consideration is the length of the seam and/or the size of the unit. This type of quilting is not as attractive for large units (for example, larger than two to three inches) as for smaller-scale units.

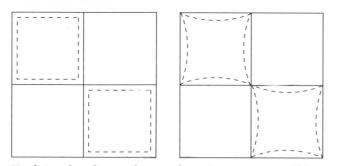

Traditional outline quilting and continuous-curve quilting

How and when you use the continuous-curve option is up to you. If you are quilting blocks where the pattern is created by the contrast of color and printed fabrics in relation to a solid background, this technique can really accentuate the image. You might quilt just the block design, possibly filling in the background with a different style of quilting. You might quilt just the background to make it recede while bringing the block design forward. Or, you might quilt every unit of the entire block with continuous curves.

a) Only blue (foreground) quilted

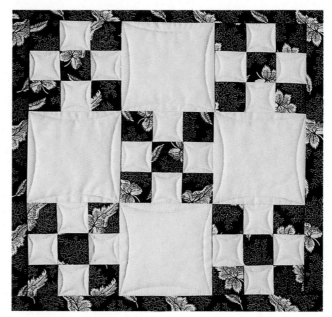

b) Only white (background) quilted

c) All units quilted

While Barbara quilted her lines with a standard presser foot, I use the darning foot, which allows me to go sideways, forward, and backward without turning and rotating the quilt. It also speeds up the process, allowing all pieces in the block to be quilted in much less time.

To use the darning foot, you must be able to control the stitch quality and movement of the quilt while going forward or backward, left or right. Not only will you be moving in all these directions and more, you will need to hit the intersecting seams dead-on. Practice this method on pieced sample blocks before working on your quilt.

CONTINUOUS-CURVE EXERCISES

Plan your block strategy on graph paper. Start at an outside corner, trace gentle arcs from corner to corner through the block, and attempt to follow every side of every piece without stopping.

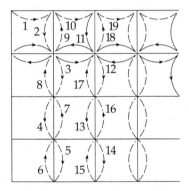

Continuous-curve system: grid

With this exercise, you'll really put your ability to quilt in all directions into practice. Follow the arrows in the example above. You'll see how the line snakes from side-to-side to accommodate each side of each piece, instead of in short, jerky, scalloped lines on the same side of each unit. This allows your hands to follow a fluid motion as you weave the line from side-to-side, serpentine-style.

Many designs require you to start in the center of the block and work in a circular manner. The following example starts inside the block and works out in a rotating manner. Follow the arrows.

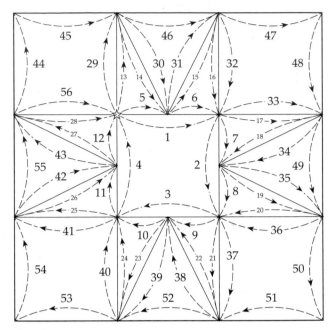

Continuous-curve system: star

In the next example, you'll quilt a long border of triangles by continually stitching two sides of each triangle, and then stitching back in a scallop motion to finish all third sides.

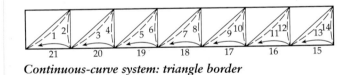

Continuous-curve system: triangle border

Finger-trace the following block patterns to get the feel for the adaptable nature of this method for quilting pieced blocks. There will be times when you'll need to start and stop the stitching, so you'll need to lock off the thread. That's okay, but try to work out a system that keeps these stops to a minimum. "Continuous" makes it faster and more fun.

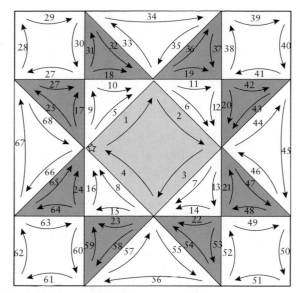

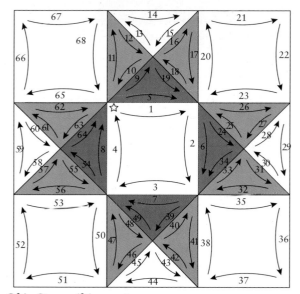

Variable Star quilting system

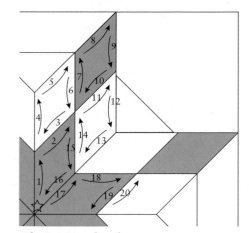

Blazing Star detail

Ohio Star quilting system

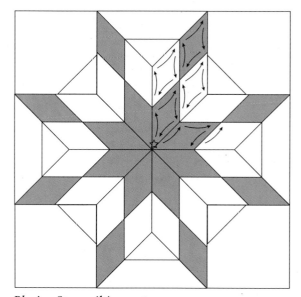

Blazing Star quilting system

MARKING CONTINUOUS CURVES

Once you get comfortable with the feel of free-motion quilting, you will be able to "eyeball" the curves and sew without marking. Until then, you may need to make a set of templates for these curves, and mark the lines on the quilt top to use as a guide. To make the templates, draw a square, triangle, or whatever shape you are working with onto a piece of graph paper the finished size of the specific shape. Use a French curve or a flexible curve to connect two corners to make the arc. Be sure that the deepest part of the arc is in the center of the line and 1/4" deep. Trace onto template plastic and cut on the curved line to create a curved template to follow. Make a complete set of templates for all the different sizes of patchwork pieces.

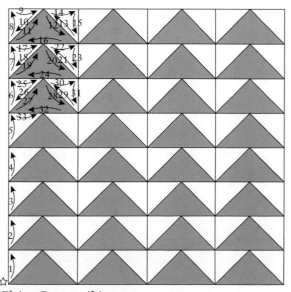

Flying Geese quilting system

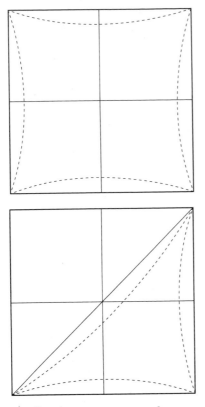

Continuous-curve templates

Another option is to mark a dot ¹/₄" from the center point at the point the line is furthest from the seam. If your needle is in the corner and your eye is on the dot, you will stitch a nice curve right to it. When you know you will hit the dot, move your eye to the next corner, and your hands will follow. Over time, you will become quite accurate with this method.

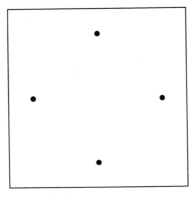

Guide dots at center points

You can also make templates to mark the dots quickly and accurately for continuous-curve quilting. Cut finished-size templates for the various units of the blocks from ¹/₄" gridded template plastic. Use a ¹/₈" hole punch to make a hole at the center point, ¹/₄" from the seam. Punch a hole in each side of the template. When you mark your quilt top, simply place the template on the corresponding shapes and mark only the dots.

Gridded template plastic for templates with ¹/₈" hole

Tip

There is no hard and fast rule that says you must stitch exactly ¹/₄" from the center of the seam. Any measurement that enhances the block is okay. On tiny pieces and unusual shapes, ¹/₈" is appropriate and attractive. If you pressed the seams open before you realized you wanted to ditch quilt them, a very shallow arc could substitute for ditch quilting without being overly obvious. If the units are large, a deeper arc would be appropriate.

Diane Gaudynski shared the slickest trick for using continuous curves to create a "wine glass" pattern for background quilting. Draw a grid of any size onto the fabric, and then quilt in the curves as though you were quilting a pieced block. When the lines are washed away, just the curves remain. No more marking with stencils, or hunting for sizes that don't exist. Thanks, Diane!

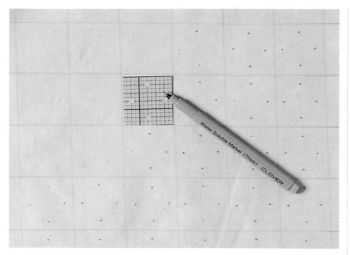

a) Draw a grid and mark curve dot.

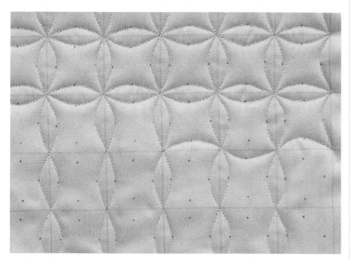

b) Stitch continuous curves into squares.

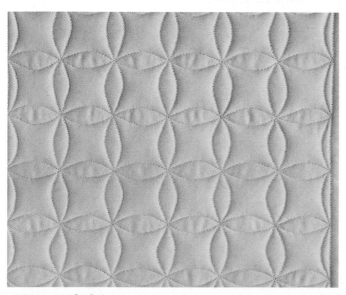

c) Lines washed away.

FREE-MOTION QUILTING STRAIGHT LINES

Many times, free-motion quilting will give better, faster results for straight lines or ditch quilting than the walking foot can give you. Keep in mind, though, that wavy and crooked "straight" lines are unsightly. If you don't have the free-motion skills to keep these lines straight and even, stick with the walking foot.

With the darning foot, you can sew forward, backward, sideways, at angles, and in any direction you need to go, without turning the quilt or starting and stopping. The seams may already be quilted, but quilting them again does no harm. I use the ditches as highways to get from one place to another without breaking the thread. It takes some practice to position the needle exactly where you want it all the time, but perseverance will pay big dividends in speed and quality.

When stitching straight lines that are closely spaced, it is easy to stitch them with a darning foot, using the edge of the foot as a guide.

When you ditch quilt appliqué with a darning foot, you will need to look both at the needle and ahead. This let's you know exactly where the needle is in relation to the edge of the appliqué, while allowing you to anticipate where you must put the needle next. After all the training you've had with the previous exercises and samples, your eyes should know to jump ahead, look at the needle, and then jump ahead again. If this is happening, you are gaining control of your free-motion quilting! This is a perfect time to use the open-toe darning foot.

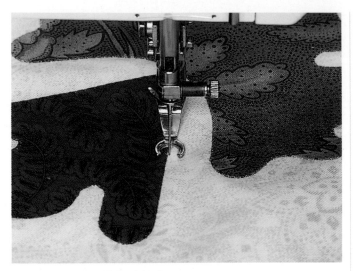

Needle rubbing edge of appliqué

ECHO QUILTING

Echo quilting repeats a shape as you move out and away from it, giving a result similar to the ripples created by dropping a pebble into a pool of water. You can space the lines exactly the same as they move away from the design, or you can space them unevenly.

This technique is used around appliqué units and quilting designs, especially feathers. It does a marvelous job of accentuating a motif as the lines repeat the shape over and over. It also makes a fast and very attractive way to fill a large amount of background area. When two sections of echo quilting merge, a secondary pattern creates even more interest.

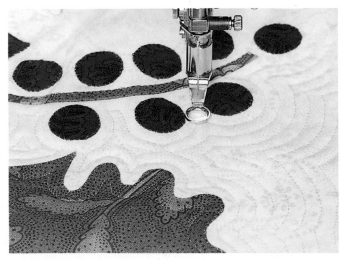

Close up of echo quilting

You'll definitely want to master echo quilting, as it refines your control. There is generally no line to follow, and you are moving the quilt in large areas in all directions to create the echoing lines. This process forces you to control the spacing, the stitch length, and your eye movement to keep everything even and accurate. It is also the basis of stippling, as you will see on page 138. Once you master echo quilting, every other form of your free-motion quilting will improve.

When you begin to experiment, you may want to draw the quilting lines lightly onto the fabric to get the feel of the design and to help you keep the spacing consistent. With practice, quilting freeform with the needle becomes easier.

PRACTICE STITCHING

Use an appliqué block with simple, small shapes to practice free-motion ditch quilting and echo quilting. Make the first echo line $1/4$" from the appliqué edge. If your darning foot is small, especially $1/4$" round, you can use the edge of the foot to measure the distance from the edge of the appliqué.

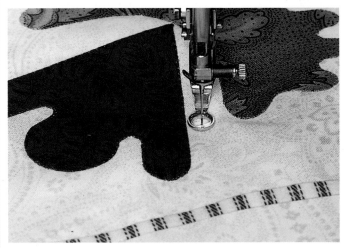

Foot placement for first round on echo quilting

Work around the design, repeating every detail of the appliqué edge. Actually rub the edge of the foot along the edge of the appliqué. This gives you an accurate and even repeat of the shape. As you come back to the beginning stitching, lock off the stitches, ending up exactly where you started.

First line of quilting: coming back to beginning

Next, move the foot out so its edge sits against the line you just stitched. This measures the next $1/4$" stitching line and expands the design.

Foot placement: second line of echo quilting

Continue this process until you are at the edge of the background piece. Echo back and forth to fill in the remaining space, retaining the $1/4$" spacing, until the entire background is "echoed." When you reach a seam, move to the next location and/or spacing by stitching in the ditch instead of locking off and cutting the thread. The seams become "highways" that allow you to get from one place to another without stopping and starting.

As you concentrate on the spacing of the echo lines, you find you aren't focusing so hard on the speed of the machine or your hand motion. You'll be surprised to find that your machine and hands are coordinating perfectly, and your stitches are beginning—magically—to even out. Relax and let it happen. By now, you'll be feeling more confident about your ability to become a really good machine quilter.

When you echo quilt numerous shapes that are not connected, echo around every item once, and then a second time. Continue until one set of echo lines is $1/4$" from the others.

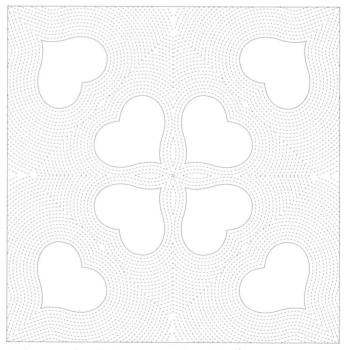

Echo around each element until lines join

Once the echo lines are equally spaced around all shapes, fill in the remaining background with consistently spaced echo quilting.

Follow the same principle for quilts with the same block repeating several (or multiple) times. The Ohio Rose quilt below is an example. Here is the order I would quilt this top:

1. Ditch quilt between all the blocks and between the blocks and border.

2. Free-motion ditch quilt around every unit of each appliqué, starting with the center row, top block. Work down the row, and then move to the row on the right. Turn the quilt end-for-end and quilt the blocks on the right of the center.

3. Echo quilt one round, $^1/_4$" from the applique edge, in the background of each block. Continue with additional, separate lines of echo quilting until the echo hits the construction seams. Quilt all blocks equally at the same time.

4. Finish the echo quilting by filling in the "puddles" left between the blocks. The echo lines work into the center of the area, maintaining the same spacing as the rest of the echo lines.

5. Quilt the grids in the borders with a walking foot (or darning foot if your skills are up to quilting very long, straight lines).

ECHO-QUILTING OPTIONS

Echo quilting becomes very refined and elegant when the distance between the lines is less than $^1/_4$". Tiny echo stitching, $^1/_8$" or closer, will give you an alternative to stipple quilting (page 137) when you want a heavily quilted background. It does take tremendous control though to keep the distances tiny. You no longer have the edge of the foot to guide you, so the control rests totally with your eyes and hands. Good visual contact is critical. You'll really appreciate your open-toe darning foot here; the open front lets your eye get much closer to the needle. Use the space between the needle and the previously stitched line to help measure the echo.

Ohio Rose quilt with echo quilting around appliqué blocks

¹/₈" echo quilting using an open-toe foot

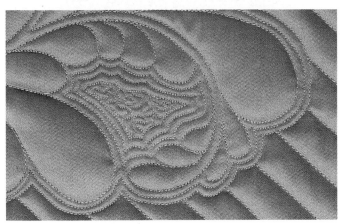

Tiny echo quilting

You can also use echo quilting to give the appearance of hand-outline quilting by quilting inside an appliqué unit or design. The photo below shows the placement of the foot ¹/₄" inside the edge of every appliqué piece. This technique adds texture and relief to the finished quilt and is fast and fairly easy to do with the darning foot.

Inside echo quilting

When you study antique quilts, you often run across examples that use echo quilting to accentuate a quilt design. Once the design is quilted, a line of echo quilting is stitched evenly around the entire perimeter of the design. This distance can be ¹/₈" or wider. Additional lines can be stitched for even more definition.

¹/₈" echo quilting used as a buffer for the design to the background quilting

Stipple Quilting

NOTE: *The words "stippling" and "meandering" are commonly used interchangeably.*

Stipple quilting is a type of background quilting. Traditionally it has been stitched by hand, and is often seen on antique counterpanes (white-work or whole-cloth quilts) of the late eighteenth and throughout the nineteenth centuries. At first the stitching appears random, but when examined closely, you can see that it is actually very close echo quilting, with about ¹/₁₆" of space between the lines. The stitching is so close that the lines appear almost to touch. It is seldom seen on today's hand-quilted quilts because of the immense amount of time needed to accomplish the process by hand.

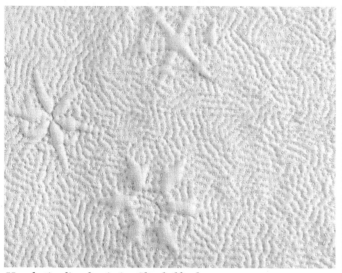

Hand stippling by Anita Shackelford

You can accomplish extremely small, close, and even stitching on the machine that truly resembles hand stippling. Diane Gaudynski calls this echo quilting with shapes. It is also called micro-stippling.

A sample of stippling by Diane Gaudynski

The photo (left, bottom) is an example of Diane's stippling. It is truly a series of echo lines building on one another around random shapes. This form of stitching gives Diane's quilts a very refined and classic appearance and is definitely a skill to strive for. For details, refer to her book *Guide to Machine Quilting*. (See page 175.)

A more commonly seen form of machine stippling is larger than the example above, and I generally refer to it as meandering. Whereas stippling gives the background a rippling effect, meandering appears more textured and wavy. Meandering usually ranges in size from "lines" spaced $^3/_{16}$" apart to very large, puzzle-shaped pieces. It appears to be random as it fills an entire area to create a fairly heavily quilted texture, but as you examine it closely, you see that the lines never touch one another, do not have points and angles, nor do they cross or look scribbled. They are very controlled, curly lines that systematically fill both large and small areas with an abundance of texture.

The true purpose of stippling or meandering is to flatten and texturize the background area around a wonderful quilting pattern, such as a feather wreath. Unfortunately, this quilting form has been taken into the realm of "mattress-pad" quilting, where the curved shapes are placed over the entire quilt surface in an overall pattern much like that on a quilted mattress pad. This is a far cry from what this stitching was originally intended to do for a quilt.

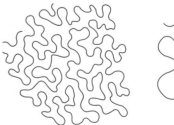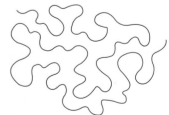

Examples of various-sized stippling and/or meandering

A sample of stippling by Harriet

The practice exercises covered earlier focused mainly on learning to move the fabric under the needle to get where you wanted to go and to execute the desired shape—hopefully with even stitches. If you are still struggling with this, and still looking at the needle or in the opening of the darning foot, you are not ready for stippling. You must be able to look ahead of the foot. Try both your closed and open-toe darning foot to see which provides you the most control and allows your eyes to travel where they need to be.

Offset open-toe free-motion foot

Due to the random nature of stippling, you need to know at all times where you are, where you are going, and where you have been. If you look ahead and all around, you can plan where to go and what you need to avoid before you get there. You never want to cross any quilted lines, create points, angles, or uneven stitches: a lot to ask for! Practice quilting free-motion and not looking at the needle or in the foot to prepare yourself to practice stippling.

For years, I have suggested that students learn to draw stippling before they try to quilt it. To stitch a pattern, you need to familiarize yourself with its various elements and how they all come together. I used to practice stippling while talking on the phone. A random piece of paper, the cover of the phone book, magazine covers—all were fair game. Whenever I came to print on the page, I would make myself work around it. I'd stipple around letters, pictures, anything taking up space. Try it: you will soon get the feel for shapes and the movement needed to go around them. You'll discover as you get a rhythm going that your stippling has its own signature. It is like handwriting—we may all be taught the same method of writing, but our own handwriting is distinctly different from anyone else's. Try as I may, I cannot get my stippling to look anything like my friend Diane's, and this is why. Her stitches are hers, and mine are mine.

PRACTICE STIPPLING

Stippling requires a lot of practice. You may need to sit with a piece of paper and doodle for a while to warm up to the motion. You may need to run the machine speed more slowly for very small stippling, and run your machine faster, moving your hands more slowly, for 1/4" and larger meandering.

Tip

If you plan to make your pattern larger than 1/4", be sure to keep your stitches small. Even though you are moving the quilt more aggressively, you'll want to maintain your hand speed so the stitches are never longer than 1/8".

Try not to get cornered when stippling background areas of blocks connected by corners and points. Plan the work so it stays random but has an entrance and exit point. Use the corners and points of the design to get in and out of an area.

Once you get to the machine to practice, there are a few basic concepts to bring it all together. To stipple well, you need to run the machine **fast** and move your hands **slowly**. When you begin to practice, it is common to move your hands way too fast, creating large, irregular stitches. Tension and fatigue will soon set in. So, take a deep breath, relax, and try again.

It is also common to repeat the same shape over and over, usually in lines. Think of a wandering river, such as the Colorado River going through the Grand Canyon. The curves are gentle and smooth, but they can turn back on themselves, and then head off in another direction, and then come back to finish filling the space. Your goal is soft, gentle, evenly spaced continuous curves—no long distances without shapes. Look at the illustration and photo on page 138 and study the patterns. Instead of repeating the same line over and over, you'll want to add a different shape now and then, like a dog bone or a puzzle piece. Try to keep shapes roughly the same size so no single shape stands out. Evenly spaced

shapes are more important than tiny shapes. Keep the stippling at a size you are able to stitch consistently. You need a good rhythm to stitch very tiny stitches, and the stitches must be very small when you do small stippling. You can't make smooth, small curves with long stitches. Keep up the speed on your sewing machine.

Needle and thread size can affect the size of stippling. When you are just beginning to practice, a size 70/10 needle with 2-ply, fine machine-embroidery thread looks very nice. The needle is small enough so the needle holes are small, and the thread is fine enough to leave a fine, smooth line. As you reduce the size of the shapes in your stippling, reduce the size of the needle and thread. Try a 65/9 or 60/8 needle with 60/2 machine-embroidery thread, 50 or 100-weight silk thread, or nylon monofilament. These tiny and more delicate threads leave tiny holes and refined-looking stitches.

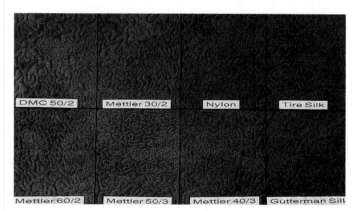

Examples of different threads on the same fabric

When stitching around any design element (for example, an appliqué or pieced unit or a quilting pattern), keep stippling in proportion to the design. The stippling should be smaller than the smallest element in the design. Begin stitching right at the quilting line of the design; for example, at the edge of a feather. As you start to go around the design, stitch right up to and onto the quilted line of the motif. You don't want any open spaces. Don't travel too far without giving the stippling lines shape. Work in small areas, fill in all the space, and then move on, blending the shapes as you go. Let the shapes echo one another, at the same time creating new ones to keep the pattern interesting.

Stitch right up to the feather when stipple quilting.

The most important thing to remember is to stay relaxed. When you feel yourself tensing up or starting to loose your focus, stop and look up, close your eyes for a bit or look outside for a minute or two, stretch, and then go back to stitching. If the stitches become uneven or erratic, it is time to walk away and come back later.

As you do more and more stippling, you'll see the shapes refine and your overall work improve. The more you stipple, the better you get. Keep stitching—and don't forget to breathe!

COMBINING STIPPLING WITH OTHER QUILTING ELEMENTS

I couldn't end this chapter without showing you what incredible textures you can achieve when you start to experiment and to pay attention to what other quilters are creating. While at a quilt show in Minnesota in 2002, I stood in front of a quilt that I couldn't walk away from. That quilt—*Treasures of Julia's Life* by Joanie Zeier Poole—appears on page 155. What struck me was the imaginative use of grid quilting in combination with stippling. Joanie quilted a grid in the inner border of the quilt, and then stitched tiny stippling in every other square. What an effect! Look at the quilt again, and study the white outside border. The fingertip shapes look like dentil molding often seen on Colonial houses: striking! Needless to say, I couldn't wait to get home and play. My attempts to explore this wonderful texture appear here. Thanks, Joanie, for the terrific ideas!

a) Quilted just as stencil was drawn

b) Enhanced by adding tiny echo and stipple quilting

Isn't this the best reason for making a quilt? Who knows about the comfort and warmth of quilts better than napping kitties?

Feathers

CHAPTER 13

Quilters have used feather designs on quilted items throughout history. Feathers come in all shapes and sizes: single, double, intertwined with cables, stylized, and continuous. I have met few quilters who didn't dream of stitching beautiful feathers on that special quilt. Nothing adds more elegance to a quilt than a feathered design.

The good news is that feathers are not all that difficult to learn. I don't suggest that you start with a 16" double-stitched feathered wreath. However, with practice on smaller, continuous-line wreaths and borders, and a few tricks and techniques, you will be quilting fabulous feathers before you know it, especially if you have taken time to practice the skills in the previous chapters.

When you look closely at the various feather patterns, you will see a lot of variation. Feathers generally have a spine (the center line of the pattern). One line or two lines may form the spine, which can be straight or curved. You can draw the feather so the spine is created by the placement of the feathers. You can also leave spaces between each feather, so the feathers don't touch and there is no spine. These are called continuous-curve feathers and are the easiest to quilt on the machine.

Look at the illustrations on page 144 to see the differences between traditional and continuous feathers. The first feather is a traditional design. It is easy to push the needle between the layers of the quilt to get from one spot to another when hand quilting. You can't do this with a sewing-machine needle.

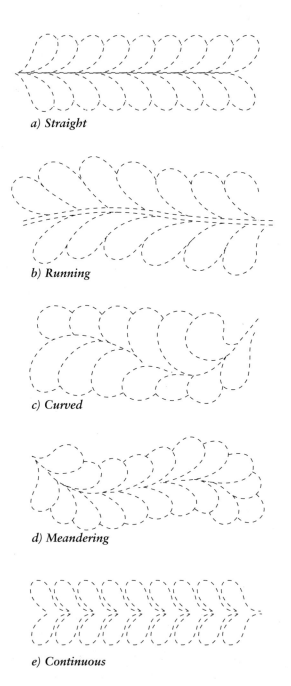

a) Straight

b) Running

c) Curved

d) Meandering

e) Continuous

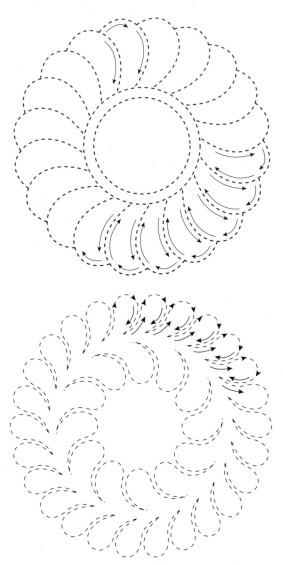

Traditional and continuous-feathered wreaths

There are two alternatives for quilting this traditional feather on the machine:

1. You can lock off the threads at the beginning and end of every design line. I don't recommend this method as it creates a sloppy backing from all the lock-off stitches and can weaken the quilting line if the thread tails are not locked off adequately.

2. You can exactly retrace some part of a line to quilt the design, and move from line to line without breaking the thread. This is referred to as "double-stitching" a line, and is the method I prefer. Optimally this stitching goes "in and out" of the same needle holes. Be patient: it takes quite a bit of practice to achieve the necessary accuracy.

The second feather pattern can be worked continuously. There is no need to restitch any of the lines. Every feather has its own in-and-out stitching line. You are going to wash away the drawn lines afterward, so you won't be able to tell if you hit them exactly or not; you still can produce a beautiful feather! You can master a continuous pattern like this one with very little practice. The more you quilt continuous-line feathers, the more you'll develop the skills you'll need for more difficult patterns.

Continuous-Line Feathers

There is a rhythm to quilting continuous feathers—much like a chant. Because you quilt only one line of one feather at a time, it's easier to keep the stitches even and smooth. Follow along on the feather below:

1. Begin stitching where the base of the feather would attach to a spine.

2. Quilt around the entire shape. When you reach the point where the next feather would join a spine, stop for a heartbeat. This stop allows the needle to take a couple of stitches in the same hole to form a sharp point. It also gives you time to plan where you are heading next.

3. Quilt the next feather, stopping at the point. Imagine yourself chanting: around the curve—stop at the point, around the curve—stop at the point.

4. Reposition your hands when necessary, always with the needle in the fabric. If you are working on a closed design, such as a wreath, quilt the inside feathers of the design first, and then the outside feathers.

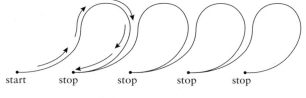

Around the curve—stop at the point.

As you quilt continuous-line feathers, remember that the lines are merely guides. If you don't hit them exactly, you probably won't notice when you wash the lines away. Your main concern is that the curves are very smooth and fluid, and that the points are sharp. Practice quilting wreaths, plumes, borders, feathered hearts, and any of the numerous other designs using continuous feathers. If you run out of designs, try adapting traditional patterns to turn them into continuous designs. You'll have plenty to keep you busy!

Turning a traditional design into a continuous design

Traditional Double-Stitched Feathers

Once you have quilted lots of continuous-line feathers, you will develop the rhythm you need for double-stitched traditional feathers. The biggest drawback to stitching these designs is—as the name implies—the need to double-stitch certain areas within the design. The length and amount of curve in the double-stitched line depends on the shape of the feathers and the placement of the spine. There are several tips and tricks for quilting these more difficult designs.

Look at the following illustrations of different types of feather designs. The first design, with its graceful and fluid lines, is one of the easier double-stitched feathers to quilt on the machine. Because of the severe angle of each feather, there isn't a true spine at all. The feathers lay on top of one another. Finger-trace the pattern to get a feel for the motion.

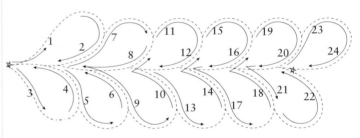

Sequence for quilting a meandering feather

1. Start at the end of the design. From the point, trace to the right, up and around the feather, and all the way back to the center; pause.

2. Trace from that center point along the underside of the second feather, around the curve, and down to the connecting point of the first feather; pause. Double-stitch on the top line of the first feather, then up and around the curve, back to the top of the second feather.

3. Double-stitch the top line of the second feather, around the outside curve, and back to the line of the third feather.

Follow the numbers and arrows to complete the pattern. Repeat the process for the feathered wreath. Once you start to stitch these feathers, you'll really get into the swing and rhythm of the curves.

Now that you know the stitching order, trace similar feathers onto a practice piece, and quilt them until you are comfortable with the hand motion.

Sequence for stitching a feathered wreath

Tip

Play with different threads and needle sizes as you practice stitching feathers. For a bolder feather, use variegated thread, or a heavier cotton (for example, 30/2 embroidery thread) that matches the fabric. For a very formal feather, try 100-weight silk thread and a very small (for example, 60/8) needle. Change the stitch length from very small to medium small for each motif. Which look do you like best? Which stitch size gives you the most control? Which thread shows the double-stitching the least?

The next illustration shows a feather with long sides on each feather unit. There is less of an angle on the base of each feather, which creates a section that is actually the spine. In this example, quilt the spine first, and then the feathers. If you plan the route carefully, you won't need to double-stitch the spine at all, and the outside curve of every other feather will be double-stitched. This technique works when the feathers are drawn directly opposite one another.

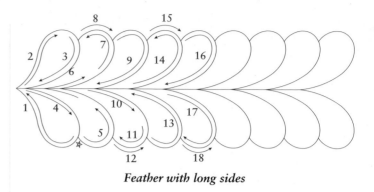

Feather with long sides

1. Start at the top of the curve of the first feather on the bottom of the spine. (See star in diagram.) Trace down toward the end of the feather unit (1).

2. When you get to the point, trace up and around the entire curve of the first top feather back to the end point (2 and 3).

3. Trace from the spine to the top of the first feather on the bottom (4), up and around the curve, and back to the spine of the second feather on the bottom (5).

4. Stitch what you need of the spine, then proceed to the curve of the second feather on the top (6 and 7).

5. Double-stitch back over the stitching at the top of the curve (8), on to the top of the third feather, and down to the spine (9).

6. Continue on in this manner, alternating between the top and bottom of the design, until all the feathers are quilted.

Tip

If you wish, you can quilt the design above one side at a time rather than alternating back and forth.

The third feathered design has a flat area along the spine. There is less of an angle on the base of each feather—a quite common way to draw feathers. The spine closes the feather shape. You quilt only one side of the feather at a time.

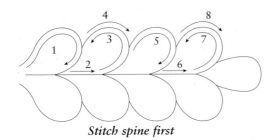

Stitch spine first

1. Quilt the spine.

2. Trace the first feather, from the end, around the lobe, and to the spine.

3. At the spine, trace backwards until you get to the top of the second feather.

4. Trace up the line of the second feather, and around the curve at the top, continuing on until the line meets the first feather. Double back on the curve and pause when you get to the intersection of the second and third feather.

5. Trace over the curve of the third feather down to the spine, and reverse direction on the spine to the line of the fourth feather.

6. Repeat until you've quilted the entire design.

In the next design, you must double-stitch in two places: at the top of every other feather, and at the base of the alternate feather on the stitching line of the spine. If the spine is a circle (as for a wreath), be very careful to stitch accurately, as a curve is easily flattened on the second pass.

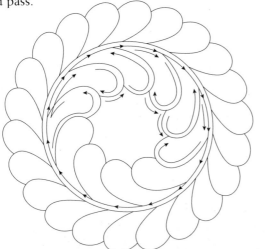

Center rings and outside of feathers are double-stitched

Another, though more difficult, approach to a feather is to double-stitch the long side of the feather after the spine is stitched. You might prefer this approach if you don't care for the look of double-stitching on the outside curve, or the buildup of thread on the spine created by double-stitching. Most quilters find it difficult to double-stitch such a long distance accurately on large feathers, but you might find you can develop a nice rhythm on shorter, smaller feathers. Try both methods to find which one gives you the most accurate results.

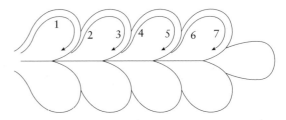

Double-stitch the long side of the feather

Tip

When planning your route for double-stitched lines, plan to restitch a line immediately after the first pass. This takes advantage of the ability of your eyes and hands to repeat the same motion accurately.

As with all quilting designs, it is easiest to start with smaller feathers while you are learning. There is more movement in the stitching, and you'll have shorter distances to double-stitch. Long, narrow feathers and graceful, teardrop feathers require longer lines to double-stitch. These are the hardest feathers to quilt.

If you are stitching a feather design in the corner of either a block or border, do not double-stitch on the outside curve of the dominant feather in the corner. This is the most noticeable feather.

Avoid double-stitching corner feather

PRACTICE STITCHING FEATHERS

Now that you understand the stitching sequence, it is time to try double-stitching some feathers. Collect a number of patterns and stencils with feathers of various shapes and sizes: wreaths, ropes, hearts, and so on. Transfer the patterns onto a large sample practice piece. Layer the practice piece, securely pinning the layers. Place pins on both sides of the spine, keeping the pins far enough away that they won't interfere with the darning foot. You'll quilt the spine first, and will probably need to stop a few times to readjust your hands. Move your hands slowly, and maintain a fairly rapid needle speed.

> **Tip**
>
> When you are first learning to quilt feathers, especially double-stitched designs, I suggest that you work with nylon thread. Nylon thread is extremely forgiving. Cotton thread emphasizes double-stitched lines—and inaccurate stitches.

Don't be afraid to experiment with various machine speeds when you are double stitching feathers. You may find it helpful to slow down as you go back over previous stitches. I strive to keep the stitches in the same needle holes I made on the first pass. I'm not always totally successful, but I find that maintaining a slower speed and good rhythm helps. Remember to look ahead all the time. If this is still a problem for you, stay with continuous feathers awhile longer.

> **Tip**
>
> When you use nylon thread, some fabrics completely hide the stitch holes made by the first line of quilting. This makes it virtually impossible to see exactly where you need to retrace. You won't be able to see anything at all on the front side, whether you restitch perfectly or not. If you stray, however, it can be very obvious on the backing fabric, so choose a busy fabric to camouflage imperfect stitching.

When you reach the point of wanting to draw your own feathers, I can recommend two excellent books on this subject: *Infinite Feathers Quilting Designs* by Anita Shackleford and *Feathers That Fly* by Lee Cleland. (See page 175.) There are also several handy tools for making feather shapes available at quilt shops. Beware: once you learn to quilt feathers, you'll be hooked on them! If the photo below doesn't inspire you to practice, I don't know what will.

Abundance, 25" x 26", designed and quilted by Diane Gaudynski, Waukesha, WI; Hobbs Heirloom Washable Wool batting; YLI 100-weight silk thread on top; 50/2 Aurifil Mako Cotton thread in bobbin.

Padded Quilting

repare yourself for one of the really wonderful payoffs of learning to machine quilt well.

Padded quilting, also known as trapunto, brings true elegance to a quilt top. The resulting dimension is simply stunning. Traditionally, the term trapunto refers to a design that is stuffed after the quilting is finished. A small slit is made in the back of the quilt and stuffing or yarn is packed into the quilted area. The tiny slit then is stitched closed. Hari Walner introduced the quilt world to a simplified machine version of trapunto in 1996.

By using water-soluble thread and an extra layer of batting, padded quilting can now be done quickly and easily on the machine. When Hari began teaching her method, she used high-loft polyester batting for the "stuffed" areas. The design really popped off the surface of the quilt. I prefer to use a lower-loft, needle-punched batting, such as Quilters Dream Poly. I find it easier to stitch around and trim away, and it is flat enough that it does not distort the block. The apparent, but subtle result gives more of a "padded" look; hence my term "padded quilting." Try different brands and lofts of batting to see which ones suit your taste. (Padded feathers are incredible! You need to try this.)

1. Thread the machine, top and bobbin, with YLI Wash-A-Way thread. Put a new size 70/10 needle in the machine, attach your darning foot, and drop the feed dogs. You may need to reduce the top tension slightly to accommodate the thread.

2. Decide which areas will be padded. Prepare the quilt top by drawing the design line on the fabric. If you plan to quilt a grid or any other background pattern around the edges of the trapunto designs, mark them before you begin quilting. The extra thickness of the trapunto batting can distort the lines if you try to mark after the padded area is stitched and trimmed.

3. Cut a piece of needle-punched polyester batting 1"-2" larger than the marked design. Place the marked fabric on the batting and pin-baste. (There is no backing at this point.)

Using water-soluble thread

4. Position the fabric/batting layers under the darning foot, and quilt around the designs that you want to be padded. Stitch slightly inside the drawn line, so that when the batting is trimmed in the next step, you are better able to complete the quilting process.

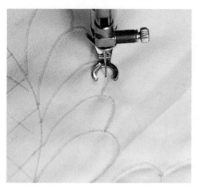

Stitch with water-soluble thread inside drawn line.

5. Once all the lines are quilted, carefully trim away the batting as close to the line as you can. Use a pair of small, well-sharpened, blunt-nose scissors. Do not use scissors with sharp points and large blades. I use a pair of "nose-hair" scissors made by DOVO. These scissors have tiny blades with bull-nose points. I can cut very close to the quilting with no fear of running the scissor points through to the front of the fabric. Working on my knee, with the fabric rolled over my fingers, I have total control of the trimming process. This is not a fast job, so settle in with a good movie or book on tape. The final product is well worth the time spent.

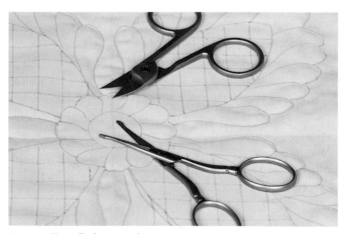

Use small, well-sharpened scissors to trim away excess batting.

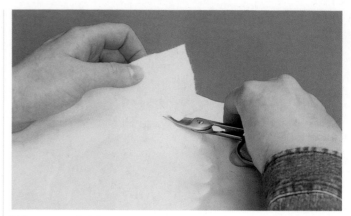

Trim excess batting.

6. Once the excess batting is cut away, layer the top onto the backing and batting as you would any quilt. Pin-baste securely.

7. Thread the machine with the thread that you wish to use for the project, and change the needle if necessary. Once the layers are under the foot, quilt all the lines marked on the quilt top. Stitch the same lines you did before, but this time on the outside of the line. Your goal is to totally encase the trimmed batting without stitching on top of its edge.

Final quilting stitched on outside of line

8. When you have finished quilting, trim the excess batting and backing as usual and bind the quilt. When you submerge the quilt in cool water, the water-soluble thread will totally dissolve.

Finished block

Tip

Just a Thought

Now that you are quilting feathers and doing trapunto work, I imagine you are grateful for all the practice time you put into learning to machine quilt. When you began this adventure, I'll bet you had no idea how much enjoyment you would derive from the process, and the satisfaction you'd get from the items you are able to produce. Congratulations for hanging in there, doing your samples, and achieving one of the most satisfying processes in quiltmaking—the quilting.

Gallery:
MASTER-LEVEL
QUILTS

Friendship Album
67" x 67", Blocks pieced by Charla Gee, Littleton, CO.
and quilted by Harriet Hargrave.

This quilt features ditch, channel, free-motion, stippling, and padded-quilting techniques. Inspired by the quilting designs of the nineteenth century. Fairfield Natural Cotton batting; Quilters Dream Select Poly batting for trapunto; Sew-Art International Invisible Nylon clear thread for the pieced blocks; 60/2 Mettler embroidery thread for the alternate blocks and in the bobbin.

Metamorphosis
*82" x 82", pieced, appliquéd,
and quilted by Jean Lohmar,
Galesburg, IL.*
This quilt features free-motion, stippling, and
trapunto techniques. Original design based
on antique Princess Feather pattern. Fairfield
Cotton Classic batting; invisible nylon
thread on top; 60/2 Mettler embroidery
thread in the bobbin.

Neptune's Garden
94" x 94", pieced and quilted by
Jean Lohmar, Galesburg, IL.
This quilt features trapunto, free-motion, echo, and stipple-quilting techniques. Fairfield Cotton Classic batting; invisible nylon thread on top; 60/2 Mettler embroidery thread in the bobbin.

Treasures of Julia's Life

67" x 80", designed, pieced, appliquéd, and quilted by Joanie Poole, Sun Prairie, WI.

Joanie created this tribute to her grandmother with wonderful texture by stitching a grid, then placing tiny stippling in every other square. Stipple quilting gives definition to the open background areas. Hobbs Heirloom Washable Wool batting; YLI 100-weight silk and Wonder Invisible Thread on top; YLI 100-weight silk thread in the bobbin.

Fields of Gold

83" x 83", designed, pieced, and quilted by Diane Gaudynski, Waukesha, WI.

The simple nature of the piecing makes a striking backdrop for spectacular free-motion quilting. All designs are Diane's originals, based on antique Provencal, Welsh, English, and American quilts. Hobbs Heirloom Washable Wool batting; YLI 100-weight silk thread on top; 50/2 Aurifil Mako Cotton embroidery thread in the bobbin.

QUILTING
DESIGNS